Living
Between
Danger
and
Love

Rutgers University Press

New Brunswick, New Jersey,

and London

Living

Between

Danger
and
Love

The Limits of Choice

Kathleen B. Jones

Library of Congress Cataloging-in-Publication Data

Jones, Kathleen, 1949–
    Living between danger and love : the limits of choice / Kathleen Jones.
        p.   cm.
    Includes bibliographical references.
    ISBN 0-8135-2744-9 (cl. : alk. paper)
    1. Family violence—United States.   2. Conjugal violence—United States.
    3. Abused women—United States—Psychology.   4. Women's rights—
    United States.   I. Title
    HV6626.2.J66   2000
    362.82'92'0973—dc21   99-26783
                                                                            CIP

British Cataloging-in-Publication data for this book is available from the British Library

Manufactured in the United States of America

*To the loving memory
of my mother, Geraldine,
and my father, Edward*

Contents

Acknowledgments

To my family, especially Amy, my two sons, Jed and Ari, and my daughter-in-law, Danielle, for the sheer joy of being in the world with you;

To my stepsisters, Susan and June, and their families and my stepmother, Carol;

To my friends, old and new, who read parts of this book and who learned to talk me through the days and nights of it and, most of all, who helped me say it right—Ashley Phillips, Mary Adams, Joanne Wells, Paul Bowers, Barbara London, Sharon McMahon, Susan Cayleff, Michele Hagan, Kathi Diamant, Gun Hedlund, Gunnel Karlsson, Ann-Cathrine Åquist, Berit Åberg, Malin Ronnblom, Anna Jónasdóttir, Ingrid Pincus, Stephen White;

To Polly Mason, for being there, then and now;

To all my "sisters" in Sweden who shared the secrets of the shadows with me;

To my students, especially Susan Chan, Jenny Johnson, and Jenee Littrell, for teaching me;

To SDSU Wormen's Resource Center, especially Hani Baumgarten and Madeline Yang;

To Kendra Gratteri for her extraordinary research help, her immense wellspring of support and friendship, and her wonderful insights into the dynamics of love and power (I can't wait for your book!);

To Andrea's family and friends, especially Lesley, for sharing their sorrows and for sharing their hopes; Lesley, dear lady, we are joined at the heart;

To Peter Gallagher for listening and for agreeing to disagree;

To my colleagues on the San Diego Domestic Violence Council;

To Senator Dede Alpert, for all she and her staff do for women in California;

To the women and men, named and anonymous, known and still hidden, whose stories are in here;

To Cecilia Cancellaro for encouraging me;

and to Marlie Wasserman and her incredible staff at Rutgers University Press for keeping me going and keeping me focused, and for believing in this project from the start;

To all these I say thanks for helping me learn that living is a sanctuary filled with all the possibility in the world.

Living *Between* Danger *and* Love

1 Between Power and Love

≈

What Happened?

In the early morning hours of November 5, 1994, a twenty-seven-year-old woman named Andrea O'Donnell was brutally murdered. Her badly decomposed body was discovered by another roommate in the apartment that she had shared with her boyfriend. A few days later police arrested Andrés English-Howard, Andrea's boyfriend, and booked him on suspicion of murder. In the late summer weeks of August 1995, after only a two-week trial in San Diego Superior Court, Andrés English-Howard was convicted of murder in the first degree in the death of Andrea O'Donnell. The night before he was scheduled to appear in court for sentencing, Andrés ripped apart his bedsheets, and, in a series of gestures that eerily mocked the way he had killed his girlfriend, stuffed a gag in his own mouth, covered his head in a shroud, and hanged himself in his prison cell.

An awful story, yes, but on the surface, nothing unusual. Andrea's story is just one of the millions of stories about women who are victims of violent abuse every year. She was just one of the thousands of women in the United States alone who, in 1994, were killed by those whom they loved and whom they ought to have been able to trust the most—their husbands, their lovers, their partners.

I knew Andrea. But what for me makes this story seem so different from all the other stories about women victims of violence is not *that* I knew her, but *who* I knew her to be.

Andrea O'Donnell, women's studies major at San Diego State University, student director of the campus Women's Resource Center, self-defense instructor, politically active and strong young woman, died in her own bedroom, strangled to death by her lover. Andrea did not fit what criminal justice experts still call the "victim profile"—a composite shot of the characteristics of vulnerability and an inability to protect one's self from danger that separates the likely "victim" from the rest of us. By any of these measures, Andrea was not a victim. Yet, she became a victim. Her death brought the reality of violence against women as close as it ever gets to the center of feminism. If it could happen to her, then it could happen to me, her friends thought. And they were right.

I knew Andrea well. Yet I came to know her even better after her death. Still, after more than four years of living with her death and the echoes of it I keep hearing in other lives and deaths and near deaths, I cannot claim to have the answer to what really happened or why it happened to her. I have stopped trying to figure out why. Instead, I have come to believe that her story has another meaning; her story has a lot to tell us about who we think we are.

To me, Andrea's story becomes a meditation on the hollowness of the word "choice." We might say that Andrea made a choice; Andrea made her life for herself. But do we really expect that Andrea, or anyone, could survive having to choose between two people, having to knowingly discard one in favor of the other? Is that something we want to call a "choice"? No, I think it's one of those all too frequent occasions in life when the idea of choice seems utterly beside the point. And I think we all really know this. I think in that hollow word "choice" we hear the echo of a nagging suspicion, a hesitation that makes us shiver with the knowledge that, even under the best of circumstances, being able to choose is not enough to get us through the night. Underneath the assertion that choice is all we need, we sense that it doesn't and can't explain why, even if we *can* choose, we should ever be expected to make choices that are *unreasonable*.

By unreasonable choices I don't mean choices without reason; I mean being unable to reason in the face of choice. Being unable to reason, you are unable to believe, once and for all, that one purpose for living is much better than another. All of a sudden all the arguments you can muster for going in one direction or another start to pull and tug at you equally and turn you inside out with indecision until you feel, quite literally, as if the edges of your world have disappeared. And you want nothing more than to be freed from having to choose at all. Tell me you haven't been there. Were you afraid to admit it?

We all find different ways to hide from such feelings. One way we hide from these feelings in unreasonable situations is to create a category like "victims." We become fascinated with "the victim," curious about how she could just let something bad happen to her. I think we want to know *why* something bad happened to her, what went wrong with *her* life, so that we can create a safe distance between ourselves and the victim who made *bad choices*. We say, well, maybe she or he would do that, or couldn't help but do this, but I—I would be different, I would know how to make the right choice, the good choice.

The trouble is, stories about "bad choices" keep getting closer and closer. They hit home. So we dig deeper. We try to find another way to build a stronger wall between ourselves and the possibility that her story, the victim's story, might really be about me, about you and me. And we're cleverer still. If the victim who made bad choices seems just like you and me, we say, well, except for that one mistake of judgment, that person is really very ordinary, very much in control, just like me.

I am no exception. At first, I saw Andrea as someone who had made a disastrously bad judgment, someone who had failed to get the help she needed. I was troubled by her not turning to us in the university for help. I thought she should have known better. But the longer I spent thinking about Andrea's life and death, the more she became for me a complex symbol of the contemporary women's movement. She was a woman struggling for justice, wanting to love and be loved. "Well, who isn't?" a friend said. Finally, through that casual comment, I recognized something even more familiar about Andrea.

When I looked again, there was Andrea standing right in the middle of my own life. It was only an accident, mere chance, that what happened to her happened anywhere near me, anywhere near my life's middle. I knew that. Still, it's hard to ignore thinking about where and who you are when things like this happen. You start thinking about where you are in your world, where you are in your life's cycle, in your thinking about yourself. And all this influences what you see and how you shape what you see going on around you. So none of what I can tell you about Andrea can be told without revealing something about myself.

Standing right in the middle of my own life, I saw Andrea as a very personal, conflicted symbol of my own womanhood. It's not that she was just like me; I was just like her. The twenty-seven years of her life spanned the length of the contemporary women's movement in the United States, the time of my own political growth. I couldn't help but see her through that history, through the history of combinations of where we both had been in those years. I saw her as the daughter I might have been.

Andrea became for me a daughter not only because her mother was my age, or even because Andrea was, in many ways, the "daughter" of contemporary feminism. For those of us who have been involved in the women's movement during the last twenty-five years, we each have had "daughters" of one sort of another. And, unavoidably, we each have been daughters during this same time.

As I thought about the new generation of women awakening to feminism in my women's studies classes or becoming involved in women's issues in their local communities—women who were different ages, came from different backgrounds, and had different values—I began to think about Andrea as the daughter that we each have been trying both to become and to avoid becoming. She became for me the daughter that I might have *had,* that I might have *been.*

As daughters, many of us have tried, each in different ways, to craft a life for ourselves that, more than anything else, would be unlike the lives of our mothers. As daughters of feminism, we often saw our mothers as the kind of women who lived confined, unfree lives. No matter who we were, none of us said, unequivocally, "I want to be just like my mother." And even when we honored our mothers' lives, recognized the complexity of their ordinary joys, their extraordinary struggles, and their unending dreams as women, we still saw ourselves as women who had more choices, more possibilities to live wider lives, than they did. When we thought about our fathers, we often thought of them in relation to our mothers or to ourselves. They were our mothers' husbands, our fathers. We may even have resented what we thought was their undeserved power over our mothers' lives, or over our own lives. We found it harder to see our fathers' joys, their struggles, their dreams. We were least successful at seeing our fathers as men—powerful but limited, stunted, confined by the culture's rules that still shape all our lives.

So we built our lives around an axis called choice. Choice became the cardinal principle of feminism. Of course, there were (and are) enormous disagreements about how limited our choices really were, or what the best choices should be. But, on the whole, we believed that we were taking control of our own destinies, that choice would allow us to coordinate every aspect of our lives. Even when we recited chapter and verse about how limited women's power to control our lives was, we still believed that knowing about these limits would set us free. Every feminist wanted to see herself as the liberated center of a world of possibilities. At least, that has been our public feminist persona.

Andrea's life and death made me wonder more about what secret and overwhelming and lonely burden that badge of proclaimed liberation carried with it. Andrea's story has forced me to examine my own complicity in keeping secrets.

I have wondered a lot about why Andrea seemed to feel the most isolated from those who presumably could have helped her best—her fellow feminists. It seemed that her sense of liberation came at a heavy price. I think she felt, like most of us do, that she should not have been having any problem with relationships at all. And she felt this for complicated reasons—she saw herself as liberated *and* as a caretaker. Even if she knew she was in trouble, she refused to accept any simple, care-less way out. She knew herself to be a responsible adult *and* an empathetic, caring person. She paid attention. She knew she could take care of herself and could care for others. This was what her feminist principles taught her. Didn't they teach that to everybody?

I'm not so sure any more. I'm not so sure that Andrea didn't feel alone and overwhelmed by it all precisely because she felt that she should have been able to handle anything. I have begun to wonder whether there has been enough public talk about the difficulty of combining power and love in anyone's life. I don't mean just pointing to examples that show how difficult and unreasonable the choices we have had to make really are; I mean doing that without saying something simplistic like "It's the system that keeps women down" or "If you work at it really hard, you'll find that balance."

Privately, most of us have confessed that we feel insecure. "If they only knew how scared I really feel . . ." But we need more public testimony about how costly an effort trying to broker power and love in anyone's life has been. Without revenge and without blame, we need to identify the costs of finding balance in our lives, and we need a way to talk about who should shoulder the burden of these costs. We need to find women and men who will say not that we are survivors, but that we were once and are still warriors, battling against anyone who forgets that we need one another, battling against our own forgetfulness.

I have had to put myself in Andrea's story not only because I knew her, but also because I have learned from her about my own struggles with similar conflicts between power and care. And, because of that, I have learned about her humanity and her desire for dignity. But I also have had to acknowledge these same things about Andrés, her lover, her murderer. I have had to confront the chilling fact that he would not remain a monster; he too had to become human, to desire dignity. In part, this was because I came to accept the fact that Andrea loved him. If I didn't accept that fact, if I said something like, well, she thought it was love, but she was confused, then I became a thief, stealing from Andrea some very large part of what she had given herself.

But the other part of recognizing that Andrés was not a monster came from seeing him in court, from thinking about what he was thinking about when he killed himself. He felt remorse. He asked for forgiveness. Letting go of the monster has been, perhaps, the most difficult lesson of all. It has meant that, finally, there can be neither victims nor victimizers in this tale.

Victims and victimizers are cardboard characters that populate the stories told in publicized courtroom dramas or on sensationalizing television talk shows about women who are brutalized by violence and about the men who beat or kill them. These images of lifeless creatures create almost unbridgeable chasms between their lives and our own. When we see battered women as pathologically weak, we secure a bearable distance between them and us. We become convinced that their portraits are not ours. To tell Andrea's story so that I would not treat her life as exceptional, I have had to feel the scratchy fabric of it rubbing on my skin.

And through her story I have come to suspect that our everyday ideas about choice are worn. Morally thin and emotionally distancing, the sad, flat, lifeless tones of our ideas about choice cannot even come close to the passionate arias of living. Andrea cannot be described, except in a distorting way, as having "chosen" to stay or "chosen" to leave. She "chose" both. When confronted with deeply conflicting demands, most women do choose both. But the conflicts that we confront are not between staying or leaving. The conflicts are about unreasonable choices, like the choice between power and love.

The complication is that if the language of choice does not work to explain how or why Andrea acted, neither does it explain how or why her lover, her murderer, Andrés, acted. If asking "Why didn't *she* leave?" keeps the conflict between power and love out of the picture, so does the question "Why didn't *he* stop?" From inside this story, I cannot find any way to say, in an uncomplicated way, that because men *choose* to use violence they can simply *choose* to stop. From inside this story, choice isn't really the issue. Not for anyone.

Our everyday ideas about choice are worn and we have nothing to put in their place. But maybe Andrea's story can help. Andrea's story holds much for me, then, both personally and politically. I have been interested in telling her story not because of how unique she is—we are each that—but because of how much she *is* each of us. By this I mean not that we are all the same but that none of us is exceptionally alone. Despite the ways in which we differ from one another, I think that the conflicts in Andrea's story transcend her own life; they represent the desire of all of us for a different future.

Care and danger, love and harm, formed the horizon of Andrea's life. It is a blend that most of us are familiar with in one way or another, not because most of us have been hurt in our intimate lives, but because all of us have felt vulnerable when we have loved. We all need *both* power and love in our lives. We need a way to find power that comes not at the expense of love, because love is our ability to be open to, and vulnerable with, and needful of, another. And we need a way to find love that leaves room for power, because power is our ability to confirm and to recognize the dignity of another person.

We need to know what happened in this story so that we can imagine and work toward a future where it might not happen again. And that, in the end, is what makes this awful tale a story of political hopefulness.

The Phone Call

I am clear about where I was when I first heard about the murder. I was sitting in my office at the Department of Women's Studies at San Diego State University. It was late morning. I didn't have to teach that day, so I was busy making lists of all the other things I needed to do: prepare for a department meeting, return phone calls, arrange appointments, write letters, the usual array of administrative chores. When the phone rang, I noticed the numbers identifying the source of the call. It was Louise Snider, from the Office of Communications. I always enjoyed hearing from her. Louise and I had been talking a lot lately about different ways to get connections working better between the media and women's studies.

We talked frequently because we were beginning to plan a year of celebration for the department's anniversary in 1995. Women's studies would turn twenty-five at SDSU in 1995. We were the oldest department of women's studies in the country. Excited by this prospect, I was aiming for a big celebration. "Let's see if we can't think strategically about getting discussions in the press about what women's studies has been, about where it's going." Later, that became the theme of the year's celebration. Later, it rang differently in my ear.

"Hi, Louise. I could see that it was you."

"Oh, you have one of those phones, too." She laughed, nervously. "Useful aren't they. Say, I have some bad news."

"What's the matter?"

"Well, we just got a call from the La Mesa Police Department. Seems they got a phone call from someone about a body found in an apartment. And they think that the body, the woman, it was a woman, they think the woman is an SDSU student. They think that the woman found murdered was an SDSU student."

"Murdered! Oh, god, that's awful. Is it someone that we know here? I mean, why are you calling me?" I could think of reasons why she'd be calling, actually. The department got calls about almost anything involving women, whether locally or internationally. If the woman had been beaten or raped, we would be getting calls for commentary about violence against women. But that was not the reason.

"Well, Kathy, this is confidential, but they think it might have been a women's studies student."

"H-how do they know that? How could that be? Who, who do they think it is?"

"Well, they found lots of women's books and some ID in the apartment that was a student's ID card—her name is Andrea O'Donnell. They think the body might be Andrea O'Donnell. Do you know her?"

People have all kinds of ways of describing shock: it's a vacant, sucked-out feeling; feeling breathless from a strong punch in the chest; feeling that your heart is beating so fast it must be shaking the whole room; feeling an overwhelming heat, and hot, hot lights in your face; feeling suffocated, feeling numb. But I think shock is a piercing sound. It's the sound of shrieking laughter coming from a fact-finding mission in your head. It makes you turn suddenly to stare in the direction of its report, and see how terrifying life can be. In an instant flash of recognition, it makes you feel intensely for a minute, and then you go numb.

"Oh, no, no, no, no . . . it can't be, it can't be, no, no, no . . ." I kept repeating that sentence, and all the while Louise kept talking.

"I guess you recognize that name."

"Louise, Andrea is the head of the Women's Resource Center. I just saw her a few days ago. I can't believe it. How do you know? Are you sure? How sure? Andrea? No, it can't be true. I just saw her. She was here in the office last week . . ."

"Well, the police are pretty sure, but they can't say publicly because they cannot identify the body for certain yet. They're waiting for the family to help. Her body was, well, it was pretty badly decomposed. She's been dead for several days. Did she drive a motorcycle?"

"Why?"

"The police said that there was a motorcycle found behind the building. I just thought maybe that would help you, you know, know more certainly. But they're pretty sure it's Andrea."

I couldn't remember for sure about the motorcycle. That wasn't the side of Andrea that I knew. I could remember Andrea visiting my office the week before, after talking with me on the phone about upcoming plans for the Women's Resource Center, about a program of music that she had been planning to help raise money for the center. And the week before that, she had been asking for the department to help fund some flyers for a visit from Patricia Ireland, president of NOW, which she had arranged.

"Andrea, I think that's great, a great idea, but we haven't got the funding here. You need to do a budget and get funding from student services. I'm sorry. You've got to ask them to support this."

"Well, OK, I just thought since it was so little money, maybe the department could help."

"We can't use the small budget that we have for this. But we will announce things that you plan in all the classes. We'll distribute the flyers."

What I remembered most about Andrea, what drew me to her, was her passion for politics. I met her for the first time in late October 1993, at a party thrown by colleagues of mine for women's studies students who wanted a more informal way to connect with each other and with their professors. For some of these students, the existing organizations on campus did not feel welcoming or accessible enough. They said it was hard to feel part of a group that already had defined alliances, central allegiances. Other, newer students, who were just beginning to discover a feminist vocabulary, wanted a low-key, less judgmental environment in which to challenge their own points of view and critique the alternatives. Their inexperience with classroom discussions seemed to be restricted further by the dynamics of women's studies. This was not because the women's studies classroom was any more controlling of students' points of view than others could be. Most college students discovered women's studies by happening into a class that fit the time and course requirement slot that they needed to fill. So they often found themselves in courses with lots of advanced students, students who had considerable familiarity with the content and the faculty. You could be just as fearful wondering aloud what sexism was in a classroom full of women's studies majors as you would asking basic questions about Avogadro's number in a classroom full of chemistry majors. The difference was that in women's studies, the issues came closer to the heart of your life, so alliances in such classes could feel tighter, more exclusionary.

It hadn't been that different, as I remembered, in the first heady days of women's liberation. We were each searching for allies. It was 1968, and I was in my third year at Brooklyn College, attending a course on labor economics, discussing theories of profit and surplus value. I had just finished reading *Capital,* volume 1, for another economics course. I had decided that, since I was never going to be the next Martha Graham, and since I didn't want to teach dance in public high school in Brooklyn for the rest of my life, I would abandon my arts major and pursue my other love, politics. So I busied myself, that year, catching up with all the requirements and collateral course work that would enable me to graduate with a degree in political science and, if I worked hard enough, maybe get me into graduate school.

I don't remember whether I had read any of the pamphlets that had already been produced about wages for housework. I must have seen some of that literature around. But, married and pregnant, I knew that the discussion about value and wages and labor left the work that I had just done at home out of the picture entirely. So when the professor was opining about how to measure gross domestic product, and what counted in its equation, I remember asking, "What about housework?"

"What about housework?" he snapped back.

"Well, what if you count the value of housework in terms of socially necessary labor time?"

"Well, you couldn't do that," he said. "Housework is not labor."

"But why not count it? Why shouldn't women be paid for it?" I really didn't know, at the time, where all this was coming from.

"Because who would pay for it? And, besides, you do it for different reasons. It's a labor of love. My wife certainly wouldn't want to be paid."

"How do you know?" I don't remember anyone agreeing with me. And the professor was really annoyed. But I didn't fit into any of the women's lib groups around at the time, at least none that I could find. Very young and very married and still very Catholic, I couldn't find any political groups that spoke my language. The antiwar movement was completely male dominated, and the childless women who belonged to it had an easier time going to meetings than I did. A couple of years later, I found the day care movement. Then everything changed.

I walked over to the group of students gathering around Andrea and watched on the edges while she talked excitedly, confidently, about her plans for the upcoming year. In January, she was saying, she would take over the leadership of the student-run Women's Resource Center. She had big ideas. There would be political events that the group could cosponsor with other student groups, workshops on helping students learn more about scholarships available for them. "The workshops will explain how to find different scholarships, write the essay, and use techniques to get the scholarships. There are thousands of obscure scholarships available, and the workshops will explain how to find them." There would be other informational sessions to increase participation. "I really like to get things organized. I think we can reach out even further than we have." She had ideas and a bubbly energy. She was magnetic. Her self-assured presence, her twinkling eyes, her eclectic dress, her long, braided and beaded red hair made for an impressive appearance. But the real strength of her presence came from the sense that you got that she knew who she was and what she wanted.

We connected. It was my second year chairing the department, and I was eager to help mentor a student with Andrea's enthusiasm for politics. It was clear she had a knack for seizing opportunities. She expressed a clear commitment for organizing students politically around women's issues on campus. I had worked well with Tae, the former student leader of the women's center, on many projects. But Tae was graduating, and so she was leaving the leadership, albeit reluctantly. Tae had had her own ideas about succession and it was difficult for her to let go. But Andrea had been persistent and, in the end, she prevailed. No matter what else might have been involved in the transition, it was clear that Andrea was going to keep the momentum going.

"So you've moved to San Diego from Santa Cruz. Quite a difference. How do you like it so far?"

"It's great . . . Well, it's very different. Seems a little harder to get people interested in politics here. The Bay Area was easier that way. But I'm excited to be here, happy to be studying in this department, and very much looking forward to taking over the WRC. There's lots to do."

We talked for a long time about lots of things, about the opportunities there were for progressive social change in San Diego, about what kind of department the Women's Studies Department was, about the weather.

"You know," I said, "when I first moved to San Diego, I thought this was a very conservative town, very much influenced by the military and the strength of the Republican Party. But really, San Diego is very complex. Things aren't always what they appear to be on the surface."

"Oh, I know, I know. It's just, well, different. So, well, you know, so sunny all the time."

That made me laugh. Everyone loves the weather in San Diego. It's always perfect, they say, a perfect climate. No flaws allowed in perfection.

I had never thought about the weather as a cultural lodestone until I moved to San Diego. That was in 1980 when, still married, I followed my second husband on his latest adventure in advanced degree getting. Mike was restless, unsettled. At the time I thought he was seeking in university degrees what he was afraid to find in relationships. And I was running out of patience. But even if I was running out of patience, I still wanted to try to make our marriage work. We had had a rocky life together for the last eight years. I knew even before we'd moved from North Carolina to California that the marriage was frail. But there was a kind of mad passion to his intellectualizing of life that I found attractive. And there was an erotic rivalry to our arguments that became addictive.

We fought about whose interpretation of Marcuse was right, about whether Freud was patriarchal, about the meaning of Heidegger's *Being and Time*. We fought about the kids and Mike's apparent biological inability to operate a washing machine or a vacuum cleaner or cook dinner or even go to the store. We fought about where we would go to dinner with our friends. We fought about his obsession with every illness in the book. But we loved each other as intensely as we fought.

I felt despair in 1980. I had finished a Ph.D. in 1978 but never published a word of it. I had moved on to other things, intellectually speaking. I was working on combining Marx with feminism, as were so many of my colleagues in those days. To make things a bit more complicated, I had resigned my tenure-track job in North Carolina before we moved. (Well, I wasn't as shortsighted as you might think. The dean of the college, pressured, I was convinced, by conservative political forces, took advantage of my request for a leave to give me a choice. No leave. I could keep my job or resign. He must not have been very happy with my political habits. Working with the newly formed National Organization for Women, campus branch, which I advised, I had brought Sonia Johnson, ex-Mormon, to the campus for an event soon after her publication of *From Housewife to Heretic*. The campus was strategically positioned across the street from the Mormon church. We got a big turnout. And, although he defended me, he must not have liked fielding complaints from the copy center for letting me print flyers for the democratic socialist club that I then served as faculty mentor. May as well give her a choice, he thought.)

So there I was, in 1980, in the middle of Southern California, a place I had sworn I would never live in, with no real job, two kids, and a fragile marriage. It wasn't so easy to figure out how I was going to survive and stay alive professionally. At least it was sunny.

I laughed, hearing Andrea's remark about the weather. "Well, even the good weather's not a *bad* thing, although, I agree, you can't build your politics around it. Andrea, listen, please come by my office and we can talk some more once next semester starts. I'd like to help you get started, offer any advice that might help you get going. It's great to meet you."

Andrea frequented the department office. Almost every week, there was Andrea in the outer office with some flyer, or some announcement, or some rally that she was planning. She had an almost messianic attitude toward feminist politics. Her student peers admired her but admitted to finding her enthusiasm a bit overwhelming at times. "I don't think I could take on what [she] had going. She took on everything. I don't know what's going to happen now," one student volunteer at WRC said later. Some folks didn't like her style. They found her too demanding, too rigid. But her fiery Emma Goldman–like dedication to a revolution of festivity and revelry really was infectious. It got people going. "Andrea was a fun-loving woman," another student remarked. "She wanted women to get together and have fun with each other. I remember a party she organized last semester. It was a Mad Hatter's Tea Party, and we could either dress up like a character from Alice in Wonderland or wear a funky hat. We all had a great time, and that's all that she wanted. Well, maybe she wanted more. She wanted women to believe in themselves."

Andrea had been in the office the Wednesday before Louise's call. I noticed her standing there in the outer office, talking quietly with Polly, the department secretary. Polly was the confidante of many students, especially those who were active or who were majors. That happens in most university departments. The administrative coordinator becomes a kind of guide or advisor to students when faculty are unavailable, or inappropriate, as advisors. But in women's studies, the nature of the confidences can be more personal. So much gets stirred up in the classroom about questions of identity, place, memory, responsibility, freedom. Yet because the classroom shouldn't be therapeutic—at least that is what we have preached and, I think, mostly practiced—the stirred-up emotions need to go somewhere else for attention. As often as not, the students create their own networks of support. But with some crises, especially those of students working two jobs and balancing their studies and their sanity on the edge of a shaky and transforming sense of self, an adult's guidance is needed. Polly was a very strong willed yet maternal kind of figure. Students trusted her to keep their confidences. They told her a lot. Andrea did too.

Andrea had been working hard on campus mobilizing discussions around women's issues in the '94 election. I knew how hard she had worked, and I felt bad about having had to veto the funding of the flyers she had needed. When Polly told me that Andrea was planning on leaving San Diego to go back to the Bay Area, after only a year at SDSU, I felt worse. Hardly enough time to get to know someone. Small twinges of guilt. So I went outside my office to talk with her.

"Hey, sorry we couldn't help with the flyers."

"Oh, that's OK. We got them done anyway. Hardly anyone came to the rally, though. Disappointing."

"Too bad. Say, I've heard that you are planning to leave San Diego. How come? You're so close to finishing."

"Well, I just think it's time to move on. I can't seem to get things working here, I mean, politically. It's frustrating. It's easier in the Bay Area. I can work better there in ways that I want to make a difference. I'm going to San Francisco State to finish up."

I remembered my own move up to and back from the Bay Area a few years back. Berkeley felt radioactive to me now. But then it held all the possibilities I had dreamed of. I could understand her dreams. I'd hoped she would find something different, what she wanted.

"Yes, it is hard to get things going here, but it's worth it. I can understand how you feel. It takes a while to adjust to the political climate here." I sensed that she had her mind made up. "Well, if there is anything I can do to help, Andrea, I have really enjoyed working with you, getting to know you. I am sorry we never had a class together. You have a lot of energy and I think you will do great things. If I can help, please call or write, OK? Good luck."

"Thanks. I will."

That was it. Good-bye.

I couldn't remember whether she had her motorcycle helmet with her.

Polly remembered. She remembered the motorcycle and much, much more. Andrea had shared with Polly her feeling that she needed to leave. She had told Polly how unhappy she had been in San Diego. And then she had started to cry.

"What's the matter?" Polly had asked her.

"Oh, nothing, nothing. Just some stuff at home. It's nothing," Andrea had said.

Polly remembered that she had been worried about Andrea. She had looked so tired. "You know, she told me she had almost no money. That she was living on rice and beans. The poor kid was struggling so hard."

They had been talking quietly about that when I had come into the room. And they continued to talk a little longer after I left. Then Andrea left, too.

Later, Polly remembered thinking that Andrea was just working herself too hard. The political work, her courses, working at two jobs to support herself. Andrea was just tired. She was just behind in her studies, overwhelmed. She needed to get away. She had decided to leave. That was what she had said. We didn't know what she was trying to leave behind, or how tired she was, or how lonely. We never knew, really. Later, this not knowing would haunt us, because of what we did not know and wished we had but, at the same time, because of what we did not want to know or have to talk about.

They're pretty sure. . . . She's been dead for several days. . . . Andrea.

"No, no, no . . ."

When I came out of my office, I needed to talk. Polly read my face. She shut the door.

"What's the matter, Kath?"

"It's Andrea. There's been a murder and the police think its Andrea, murdered. That was Louise Snider who called. They think Andrea has been murdered. There's a body in a La Mesa apartment. Oh, I can't believe this. Oh, god, oh, shit. Where did Andrea live? Did she ride a motorcycle?"

"What! In La Mesa. And, yes, she did. What's going on? How do they know it's Andrea? Who did it? What happened? Andrea? I just saw her a few days ago . . ."

Then the phone rang again. When I finished the conversation I listened to all the other messages I had stored. One was from Andrea.

"Hi. it's Andrea. I just want to let you know that I made all the reservations for the rooms in Aztec Center and Scripps so that we would have the spaces for the lecture series, if you need them, just in case. OK. Bye, now." It was from Friday afternoon, the week before. Later that same night, she was already dead.

The day of Louise's phone call swelled into something I couldn't recognize, a storm of violence I had never been that close to before. I didn't want the dead woman rolled up inside the mattress, with a plastic bag over her head, and a cord wrapped around her neck, I didn't want that dead woman to be Andrea. But who could I possibly want it to be? I called the Women's Resource Center. No one had seen Andrea, people were waiting for her, they were confused by my call. I said it was nothing, don't worry.

I don't know exactly the sequence of events after that. I know I spent the night watching the TV news reports. There was an announcement of the discovery of the body. But no identifying information. I called my colleagues, two friends who I knew had been close with Andrea. I asked them about the motorcycle. They remembered it.

"But Andrea's coming to our class tomorrow, to give a report," Mary said.

I don't remember sleeping.

I might have remembered where I was sitting when I got the phone call, but I still have to reconstruct the week backward to get to the day itself. Maybe it was Monday? No, it was Tuesday. It was November 8, 1994. It was a Tuesday. I know that because Thursday, November 10, 1994, was the day the La Mesa Police Department press release identified the murdered woman: "At 1100 hours positive identification of the victim was made by the San Diego County Sheriff's Laboratory using fingerprint comparison with the Department of Motor Vehicle records. The Medical Examiner's Office has authorized release of the victim's identity: Andrea Louise O'Donnell, 27 year old WFA. O'Donnell resided at 5708 Baltimore Drive, and attended San Diego State University."

Even as I hold this paper in my hand now, a fax sheet yellowed around the edges, I think there must be some mistake. I stare at the name, disbelieving, wishing to be relieved of the knowledge that I have.

And the day before that was a Wednesday. A teaching day, but I couldn't face the class I was teaching on women and politics. Later in the week, the director of Counseling and Psychological Services came with me to class, not only to help the students, many of whom had worked with Andrea, but to help me get through a "discussion" of what was happening. It was a troubling experience. Young men and young women, older men and older women, all sorts of different cultures, different experiences, each trying to come to terms with the fact that this was a painful situation for many people in the class but, dammit, the guy was innocent until proven guilty, this was America, right, and why didn't women stop taking it, why didn't they leave? She should have known better. Will we still have the test as scheduled?

The phone kept ringing. I had made lists and lists of contacts by then. The police detectives investigating the crime scene, things the police needed from the Women's Resource Center, students who had called, media reporters, the psychologists and ministers who were on call for family and friends. I had spent the morning talking to the police, holding off the media, and writing a press release.

"You better be prepared to deal with the media. I suppose you could just say No comment, but I think it's better if you say something," Louise advised. So I drafted a statement. How do you put grief and ideology into the same sentence? "We are shocked and angered by the violent and senseless death of Andrea O'Donnell. Andrea was a Women's Studies major at San Diego State University and director of the WRC. . . . Everybody who knew her was affected by her warmth, her energy, her commitment to bettering the lives of women. She was particularly concerned with the terrible reality of violence against women."

The phone kept ringing. The day wasn't itself; it was endless hours of some poor excuse for a day. The police called to say they were still waiting for a forensic pathology report that would ascertain cause of death and confirm the identity of the deceased through her dental records. Then the official announcement would be made. "Hold off anything until then," the police said. "Yes, we know who this is. But just wait."

"Why do they need her dental records, was she beaten?" Polly asked.

"I don't know, her body was badly decomposed. It was wrapped up in the futon and left for three days. Plastic bag around her head, tied with a cord around her neck."

"That bastard, I hope they get him. Where is he?"

By now we knew that Andrea's boyfriend, Andrés, was the key suspect. Andrea/Andrés. What strange mocking was that? Their names were so close, twin sounds your mind slurred easily together into one rhythmic syllable of pain. Andrea . . . Andrés, Andrea's Andrés.

"The police don't know for sure. They think he headed north."

Slowly the students were assembling quietly in the hall outside my door. They sat on the floor, propped up against the wall, clutching their backpacks, waiting for the magician, waiting for comfort to come.

Then Lesley called, Andrea's mother. We talked for a long time. She told me she had talked the night before with "Dre," Andrea's boyfriend. It was the first time he had ever called her. He had called her collect.

"He said to me, 'I think I've hurt Andrea. We had a fight. I think I hurt her pretty bad.' And I said, sarcastically, 'Oh, is she bleeding?' And he repeated, 'I think I hurt her pretty bad.' I stopped talking then. And then I asked him where he was calling from and he said, 'It's not important.' And I said, 'If it's so important to you that you called me, why don't you hang up and call Andi and apologize to her.' And he said, 'I can't. I didn't mean to hurt her that bad.' So I said, 'Why don't you call your mother?' and he said no, no he didn't want to; he just needed to tell me that he had hurt Andi. And then I said, 'When did this fight take place?' and he said, 'Friday night.' And I said to him, 'Dre, it's Tuesday night now.' And then I said, 'Why don't you give me your mother's phone number?' And he gave me some number.

"Then I said, after he mumbled that he was really sorry, I said 'You need to tell this to Andi.' 'I can't,' he said. 'I hurt her real bad.' And so I said, 'How bad is bad?' And he said, 'I think I broke her neck.' I said, 'Are you trying to tell me that you killed her?' He repeated that sentence again, 'I'm sorry; I didn't mean to hurt her.'

"And I told him I needed to get off the phone. I still didn't believe him. I asked him once more to tell me where he was, and he said, 'I'm in a Holiday Inn on Broadway in San Diego.' I told him to hang up and go to the apartment and talk to Andrea about this. I told him I was hanging up. Then I called the apartment and Magner, the landlord, answered. But they had already found the body. Dre must have been calling me from somewhere else. The police were already trying to get in touch with me."

"Lesley," I say to her, "I don't know what to say or what to do. We are so shocked, so hurting, but you, how you must feel. What do you need?"

"Oh, sweetie, I'll be OK. I just want them to catch him, to bring him in, to put him where he belongs. And you know, I really want to have the memorial on campus for her. She was so happy to be there in San Diego with you women. She had so much to give."

"I know, I know."

"Can you do that, can you have the memorial on the campus? She'd like that. I'd like that. I am leaving for San Diego tomorrow. The police need me there and I am bringing Andi's dental records."

"Oh, I know they haven't announced it yet, but I thought they knew for sure that . . ."

"They know. They just need these things for the official report. It was her. All her things were there. Her books. I have to get the dog. The poor dog. She loved that dog. Can you help with this?"

"Yes, of course, of course. We'll take care of it."

And then she told me who was coming into town and when, on what flight and where they were staying. She told me how to get in touch with her sister Cathy in San Diego and that her sister Patty and her husband were driving down from Oakland. Andrea's sister, Laura, was in Seattle. "Thank god I have her!" She would fly in from Seattle with family friend Claire. Sister Claudia would bring Grandma Irene into town the same day. Brother Bruce was flying in from Alaska. Andi's friends—Bethany, Deidre, and Mike—were driving down from the Bay Area. Andi's daddy, Jack, would be arriving in town any moment.

"Let's make the service on Saturday, OK?"

"OK, Lesley."

"Take care, sweetie. I love you."

"I love you too, Lesley." And there was not one thing odd about telling someone who I did not know at all that I loved her, that I felt a love that came from a shared pain, a shared power, and—I don't know what else to call it, so I'll call it careful kindness. And, yes, it also came from fear, and guilt, and all of the other odd mixture of threads that I found available and used to sew up an aching heart and connect it to another.

So I made a list of all these names, this complicated family tree of scores of relatives and friends from Lesley's life, from her eight siblings and their families, from Andrea's birth parents, and from the dozens and dozens of folks in Andrea's life with whom Lesley had generously populated it through her life's arc across the country, and up and down its coasts. She was, she told me later, following the compass of care that directed her to work and to bring into the wide berth of her life so many stray animals and children and people who needed attention. A big place for a little girl. And to this list I added Andrea's own multiply skeined connections to a whole pattern of people who called me day and night to tell me different parts of Andrea's story. They made her world wider still.

Suddenly all these people had come into my life all at once so fully and so forcefully that I felt I knew them before I had even met them. I know we say that all the time; it's an easy way to express familiarity. "I feel like I already know you." But really, I *knew* this family so well from Lesley's long descriptions of them on the phone that when I saw them in person at the memorial service a few days later, I recognized almost every one. And, of course, only later did I realize how much this recognition came from other parts of my own life, its gaps and fissures. And they each recognized me.

So maybe that was why it was so hard for me to comprehend my colleagues' hesitation at the suggestion of our organizing the memorial on campus.

"Well, I know, Kathy, but where will it stop? Why don't we just take up a collection and let them make some more private arrangements."

"Because this is what the family wants. They want to be with us. And there are also the other students to consider. They need it too."

But that was only part of the story, because, of course, so did I. I needed it. I needed some closure.

Earlier on Wednesday, the police had called asking for Moya, a friend of Andrea's who might be able to help them locate Andrés, who was still at large. Moya turned up at the office. Evidently the police had found her phone number in Andrea's things, had called her, and she was hysterical. She came to the department because she didn't know what to do. Moya and Andrea were pals from way back. They did crafts work together, had gone to the women's music festivals to sell their beads and things, and had planned a trip—"a road trip for just us girls"—that they were going to take later in the year. Moya knew Andrés. Few of us even knew that Andrés existed in Andrea's life. Moya knew him from when she had met Andrea in Santa Cruz.

"I didn't like that guy. He tried to pull that black thing on me, didn't trust him. I told Andrea to watch it with him. He tried to play up to me, you know, us both being black and all, me being a sister. But I didn't trust him."

"Moya, was Andrea in trouble with him? Did he try to hurt her in any way that you know, you know, did he ever hit her?"

"No, I don't think so. But, you know, they would have their arguments, and she wasn't afraid to confront him. I mean she'd get right up in his face and stand him off. I said, 'Girlfriend, you watch that. Don't be pushing him around. He's a big guy. He may push back.' But she wasn't afraid. She'd tell him off, tell him what she thought if he was fuckin' up and shit. Oh, god, I don't know what to do. I don't want to talk to the police."

"Moya, I know you don't, but if you think there might be something that you know that can help them find him, don't you want to do that?"

"Yeah, but . . . I don't want to go talk to the police."

"Listen, I can't leave here right now, or I'd drive with you, but maybe someone else can. Maybe Polly can."

Moya sat for a long time. We talked. Then she said she was ready to go. Polly couldn't take her to the station so we asked Mary Kelly, another professor, if she could help. Mary knew Andrea well. She had been expecting Andrea to give a presentation in her class that Wednesday night. Like most of us, she was in a state of shock and anger. Mary drove Moya to La Mesa. I went back to planning for the memorial and getting ready for the next day. Whatever Moya said, it must have confirmed what the police already knew.

"It was a good thing I helped her get there, " Mary said when she came back to campus. "I'm not sure she would have gone on her own, but the cops said that her testimony was important to the case."

The next day, Thursday, the press release hit, and all the chaos that my lists had kept at bay came rolling in. Besides identifying Andrea O'Donnell as the twenty-seven-year-old white woman found dead in her apartment, they mentioned that the key suspect was in custody, Andrés English-Howard, a thirty-year-old African American man. He had run out of town, gone to his mother's in Santa Cruz. He turned himself in. But he denied he killed his girlfriend. Said he ran, scared.

The press was all over the place, including the Women's Resource Center. I had prepared myself for the questions I knew I would get: How could this happen to someone like Andrea? Did any of us see that she was in trouble? What should we be doing about this problem of violence against women? I had my pat answers to those questions, sound bites that I hoped would at least mitigate the more sensational headlines. I hadn't prepared myself for the fact that when the cameras stopped rolling two of the three reporters who covered the news during the first few days, both women, told me they wanted to cover the story because of their own experiences. One said, "I was crying on the way over here. The cameraman looked at me like I was nuts. I said, 'You don't get it, do you?' He didn't know what to say."

Students turned up at the office, dulled with pain, disoriented and with nowhere else to go, sobbing. "How could this happen? We just saw her. We didn't know anything." By then it was clear that, like it or not, this was something the department had to deal with. We knew that we needed to provide professional help for many of the students beyond what existed on the campus. With several women counselors who worked at a local shelter for victims, we planned a meeting at a colleague's house for Friday night, the night before the service. Forty people came to the meeting, all desperate for an answer, for some clarity in their memory, for a sign of what to do, for closure. The emotions ran the gamut from horror to pain to anger to guilt.

But the memorial did not bring anything like closure or solace or peace. Instead, it conjured up the ghosts of all the Andreas who have ever lived. I heard their giddy voices echoing down the corridors of my little girl's soul and colliding with the other sisters hanging out there, laughing with all the ghosts of all the dead.

I can still hear them. Sometimes—now I know that you will think this is strange—but sometimes I think that I have seen Andrea again. And then I realize that those wild red curls on the head of some young woman I happen to pass on the street, or the funny combination of camp and vamp in another's costume, or the starkly angular curves on the letter Y of another's signature, or the leaflets stacked outside the department office like talismans, those are only memory tricks of my mind, fooling me with their shadow patterns. Tricksters, they mock me. They say, No, of course, she is dead. But you, you are still alive.

Mothers and Funerals

It was the oddest experience, but at the memorial service Lesley seemed somehow positively buoyed by the whole thing. She stood at the entrance to the large assembly hall on campus that we had booked for the service and smiled and hugged each one of the people who came to share in her grief. I didn't know then what I know now. No one did.

"Hello, Amy, I've heard so much about you. Thank you for coming. Oh, hello, Madeline. Oh, look, you have one of those bracelets on that

Andrea loved to make. Did she give that to you? Oh, Joy, hello! I know you so well from what Andi told me about your work at the center. Thanks for coming."

I could see that the students seemed unnerved by all this happy, hugging recognition. The image of Lesley standing at the doorway, rubbing Andrea's worn teddy bear, with the memorial music playing softly in the background, and with all the whispered words humming around the edges of the room; the displays of Andrea's handicrafts, photos of Andrea arranged prominently along the front wall—I could see that all this was too much for them. It was not what they were expecting.

"This is really weird," Polly said to me. "Doesn't she get it?"

Still, I thought I recognized that Lesley standing at the doorway, that mother greeting mourners, needing to make everyone comfortable, needing to make everyone happy, needing to keep away the terror that would surely open up the minute she stopped what she was doing.

I had seen the early signs of denial setting in the day before, when Lesley and I spent the morning in my office, going over arrangements for the service. Even then, Lesley was cheerful. I picked up the telltale signs of excess adrenaline working on her only because I was suffering from those same bodily rushes that trick you into thinking, "This is a game, a sad game. But, soon, it will all be over, and then everything will be OK."

I had busied myself over the last few days doing the things that kept me sane. I made lists and lists of people, places, things to do. I would look at these and say my prayers to the god of order. In those lists I found a peace that others could not find, a way to bracket out the ugliness of what had happened and think about what might still be. Lesley's cheerful immersion in greeting her daughter's friends was mirrored in my lists. Both acts kept the horror at a distance. Later, Lesley would write, in an open letter to family and friends, about her feelings about November 8, 1994—the "day I was told my Andi Louise was dead. Since that moment, my whole world and all who are in it look different, sound different, and thus I confess, I am here wildly spinning for control and understanding."

Yet on the day of the memorial, the only way she could find to show how her world looked and sounded different was by being the most different mourner of all, the mother who seemed the happiest, the most caring, to have everyone there to celebrate her Andi Louise.

So the cruel, critical tongues were wagging, saying, Well, if that's how Lesley acts, it's no wonder that Andrea . . .

I didn't know then what I know now. No one did. I didn't know that Lesley had decided to focus on the one true thing that she could save from Andrea's life and death in San Diego. She had chosen to focus on Andrea's women friends in San Diego; she had turned to them and asked with her smiles for their help, asked them to anchor her in place, to help her breathe for just long enough to find her way in and through one more day.

But even then I wanted to shout, You there, so sure you know what you are seeing, tell me, where are the rules written for how mothers are supposed to deal with loss? Do we get those rules from the mothers of murdered children? Do we find them in the books about mothers who have felt so lost and alone in the world that the only way they could find to save their children was to send them away, to let them go? Maybe those mothers have the answers, the rules for how to mourn. No, you don't think so; no, of course not. No, you think it must be only those mothers over there, the ones who are crying, hiding in the corner, the ones who wear their pain on their sleeves, who act like good mothers, obviously hurt and letting you know it, it must be only those mothers who know what loss really means.

During the service I thought about the eerie poem about a mother's heart that Sara Ruddick quotes in her essays on mothering. It's a poem about a son whose jealous lover has demanded that the son cut out his own mother's heart and bring it to his lover as a testimony of his perfect love. The son complies. But on the way back to his lover's house, he trips, and drops the heart. "Oh, dear," the mother's heart says, "are you all right?" Well, isn't that what you'd expect?

In my own thirty years or more as a mother I still haven't figured it out. How to hold on to my own children, skin to skin, life to life, tight as a drum until they and I were really ready to let go. Let go of one another and find our way, sometimes alone, sometimes together, in and through the mad, mad world. Mothering is never an ending business; it doesn't come with directions for how to find the place you reach, finally finished, and say, There, that was good enough. And if I had had to let my own children go, or had my child ripped from me, as Lesley did, not just away but away forever, what would I have done? With death sitting nearby, unperturbed, would I have wanted to be a survivor, still inquisitive, still unsettled, or would I, too, have needed to escape?

Always carefully concerned, Lesley was always mothering. But below the surface of her cheerfulness was a rage too hot for her to touch. Later, at the trial, Lesley expressed that motherly rage. "It's the anger and the rage that keep me going," she said. Referring to Andrés, she continued, "I don't want that clown out there harming any other woman's child." When Andrés was convicted of first-degree murder, Lesley said, "I'm glad the jury saw it that way." But she added, "I also feel very, very sad for his mom because she has a convicted murderer for a son and that's a terrible thing for a mother to carry with her." And she meant it, for reasons I didn't know then. But people didn't like that either. They winced again.

After Andrés hung himself, Lesley had to deal with another motherly dilemma—some part of her must have known that his conviction for her daughter's death had to have contributed, even in some twisted way of his own depression's making, to his own death. His own act would return him to Andrea again and again; always she would be in the center of that darkening room where he killed her.

That fact kept going round and round in my head at the trial. He killed her, he killed himself. He threatened to kill himself, then killed her, then killed himself. She decided to leave, she tried to help him, he threatened to kill himself; despairing, he killed her, then killed himself. Only a few words' difference, only the moving around of a few verbs, to break the cycle of violence. When the words stopped whirling like dervishes, one mother's loss was supposed to equal another's. What kind of weird calculus was that? "I really feel for the family," Lesley said. And she meant that too. She knew about that too.

More than two hundred people assembled for Andrea's memorial service. It was the first of five memorial services held for her around the country. Linda Stowell, a Unitarian minister who was a dear friend of another colleague, and who had the grace and sensitivity to write a ceremony that kept to the family's wishes for something "not really religious," began with a blunt statement of fact. "Andrea is dead. You and I are alive ... We would make this hour love's hour, and these simple rites love's confessional. For it is love's tribute that we come to offer here today. Our voices may be the voices of sorrow, but the language after which sorrow gropes is the language of love."

Then slowly, one by one, the fragments of Andrea's life came forward to speak in the persons of family and friends from all over who had come to share what they knew, to witness the event, to try to heal one another.

Many of us heard about and saw sides of Andrea that day that we never knew existed. In class, she had been an outspoken leader in discussions, always the one who "had something insightful to say about the readings." The Andrea that we knew best was the Andrea who was on the "front lines" of feminism, the one who had "hope, strength, and passion for what was right and good." We knew almost nothing of Andrea's private life.

Now, other sides of Andrea came into focus. They were boldly reflected in a display of memorabilia her mother had brought from home, and heightened by the words of speaker after speaker from parts of Andrea's life not ordinarily conversant with one another. It was as if Andrea had conjured the spirits to assemble and speak in tongues. Together they provided cacophonous evidence of the personae of Andrea: the pictures of her as a girl with her many pets; the photo of her in an outdoor shop demonstration, poised on a wooden pallet that raised her just high enough off the ground to hit the anvil forcefully with her heavy sledgehammer; fashion photos of Andrea dressed in any number of haute couture outfits; Andrea standing by the Santa Cruz coast, her normally flowing red curly hair twisted into "dreds"; Andrea proudly displaying her crafts—her silver mermaid pins and multicolored beaded bracelets; Andrea in camping gear and Andrea in vamping gear; Andrea posed before the Women's Resource Center sign; and baseball-capped, T-shirted Andrea, tired smile on her face, birds-eye camera-angle framing her one more time in the room of the student center where she had hidden her backpack of belongings and slept away from her boyfriend on nights when it got too difficult at home.

Andrea kept the many pieces of her life apart from each other. When they all came crashing together in the time after her death, she had provided us—we who care about talking about the complexity of women's lives and who believe in the need to get beyond simple dichotomies—with a picture whose depth of view, angles, and shades we need to read and read again.

What emerged in the portraits that family and friends painted of her was a young woman trying to reconcile parts of herself that did not seem to fit with an image of herself that she was constantly reinventing. "She was embarrassed she didn't have full control. . . . She was supposed to be a role model. It's sad that she felt she didn't deserve extra help," one student said. She was struggling to be both multidimensional *and* consistent.

Another student wrote later about how she remembered Andrea. "It was so clear that she wanted to help others and that she stood for what was right, and cared enough to see it through. . . . I remember one night in class she was telling us how she worked at the Street Scene concerts downtown and that she confronted a man for yelling uncontrollably at his girlfriend. When he left she said she just hugged the girl and wanted her to know that she was there for her and was going to see that she was OK and safe. . . . Andrea was there for that girl and supported her in time of need. It was both encouraging and comforting to hear this story from her and to know there are still people out there who care for one another—even if strangers."

Two weeks before she was killed she had participated in a class visit to an exhibit of photos about domestic violence, *Living with the Enemy,* at a downtown art center. She talked about it later in class as a moving experience that reaffirmed her feminist convictions.

Linda ended the service with a call for remembrance: "Andrea's death is separation. . . . It is not an end to love. . . . Let us remember Andrea by living with keenness and gracefulness and caring. Let us honor her legacy by giving ourselves more deeply to life in the future—by protesting with our hearts and minds and voices every act that harms or demeans another person. . . . Let us each consider how we can carry her light into the future by working for the causes she believed in. What can each of us do to carry on the struggle against violence and human suffering?"

Outside the hall, while we exited quietly, the news media assembled for questions: "Why wouldn't someone as powerful as Andrea be able to protect herself; why didn't she leave?" I took a deep breath and answered one more time.

Another Time

I remember clearly the day that I saw Nelson Mandela in the Oakland Coliseum: June 30, 1990. I remember it as much for the event itself, and the overwhelming power of the past and future before us, as for the fact that I felt so dirty and hot and undeserving to be there. "Mandela! Mandela!" The crowd was wild with joy. Freedom was being celebrated in the hot sun of a Sunday in June, the deserved victory of decades of struggle, and here was I, cowering cowardly, embarrassed by the bruises from being beaten by the man with whom I lived, a man I barely respected any more, a man I guessed that I really didn't know, couldn't have loved. Because if I had loved him, how could he have hurt me even this once?

In the middle of the night I am awakened by his snoring. No sleep again unless I leave our bed and go into the other room. I spread out the sheets, arrange the pillows, and, stretching out on the couch, I fall asleep. I am dreaming, of what I can't remember. Loud noise of footsteps in the hallway. The door to the room is opened and slammed. And then he is on top of me. I am being beaten all about my head and shoulders. I start to shout, to reach out, to punch the air. I can't make it stop. Fists punching my head and shoulders. And then I feel myself melting, melting into nothing. If I relax, the punches don't feel so bad. I go into another room in my mind. From there I can hear him shouting obscenities, garbled phrases of accusations I don't understand. I reach out from that room a long distance above and behind me to grab his hair, fists full of hair, and, pulling the hair, I force him off me. Or, anyway, he stops. I have fists full of his hair in my hands. I want to pull his hair out. Pull his head off. I punch his head. Beat my fists into his head. And then he collapses onto the couch, arranges the sheets around himself, and falls asleep.

I run into the night to a friend's house. She comforts me. Calms me, holds me in the circle of her arms, and I fall asleep. But I return to him. It's two years before I leave him.

One year after this singular night, a night I marked in my journal with an abbreviation only I can decode, I am in an El Salvador jail. I have been arrested along with my friend, the same woman who calmed me to sleep the night of the beating. We were traveling with other friends toward a small village where we were to interview women activists. Detained by government troops that we had passed along the road in the middle of the night, we are sent back to San Salvador for interrogation. Entering the jail, I enter that same place of terror from that night a year before. I curl up on the floor to sleep. And I feel myself melting, melting into nothing. I lose all sense of time, of having a body that I care about, of being embodied. But this time, I am not beaten.

And when we are released, that same man calls me to say he's so happy I am alive. We should get married, he says. He probably means it. One year after that, I leave.

I have, by now, read shelvesful of books about violence. I have participated in dozens of meetings with various advocates and concerned citizens trying to stop violence against women in various places around the world. I have listened to a litany of explanations based on psychology, biology, sociology, or politics, describing every imaginable theory in the world. I have heard the allegations that feminists plot to exaggerate the incidence of violence against women in order to support our own sinister but self-defeating narratives about the evil of men. I have given dozens of speeches about violence and heard scores more. I continue to do all these things.

Still, Andrea's story has helped me to face exactly what many feminists, myself included, have been trying to avoid—the limitations of our vocabulary for describing either women's or men's lives. I believe that our ideas about choice, or even about resistance and empowerment, fail to express or explain anyone's life in all its complexity. That is perhaps inevitable. Things are always more complicated than they appear.

But if we really believe that things are more complicated than they appear, where will that leave us? How will we know how to assign blame? How will we be able to understand responsibility? How will we define what we mean by freedom? In what kind of world will we be living if we abandon the old ways, or even the new ways, for distinguishing between monsters and saints?

I think that the world we enter when the monsters are exorcised and the saints are resting safely in their celestial habitat is a human world. In it, power and love are more like one another than they seem. But that is not a bad thing. Power and love are life forces. They reflect our connections to and need for others in our life; we need them both so that we can become the strong and caring persons we really want to be.

Yet to reach that more human world, we have to go back into the courtroom and watch who people are and how they treat each other in the stories that we tell in court. If we watch carefully in court, we may be able to see that, although we need to find someone guilty and someone innocent, someone responsible and someone hurt, although we need to punish the guilty and protect the innocent, we also need to find another way to rebuild our relationships and our communities.

Blame, punishment, and revenge are understandable principles in court; but to act, to be, human, we have to be able to change and to forgive.

2 Courts of Martyrs and Monsters

~

Intent to Kill

This is a murder trial, folks. Cold-blooded murder. The prosecution will show how this man, Andrés English-Howard, willfully and forcefully choked Andrea O'Donnell to death. He choked her to death with his bare hands. It was not a quick kill. . . . Dr. Bonnell's testimony about the autopsy report will tell you what a long time and effort it takes to choke and strangle someone to their last breath. . . . Andrés English-Howard is not an addict. There is no believable evidence to show that he was under the influence, high, when he choked Andrea to death. . . . Andrea's friends and family will testify. Her mom will tell you about how he called her up and confessed. Later, he tried to say, "some other dude did it." That's his story, his modus operandi, he's been using it all his life. . . . He's a con man, been conning all his life. . . . The prosecution is asking for you to bring back a conviction of murder in the first degree.

—PETER GALLAGHER, *for the prosecution*

It's hard to present the story of the life of a man who took another's life. His is a life of pain, of loss, of love. No one will tell you that Andrés English-Howard did not kill Andrea O'Donnell. But neither will anyone tell you that Andrés did not love Andrea. The issue is this:

Did Andrés English-Howard intend to kill Andrea O'Donnell in the early morning hours of November 5, 1994. . . . He used drugs, it got worse in San Diego. . . . He smoked crack the day he killed her. When he got home, she was waiting for him. He heard her yell at him. He wants her to stop, to stop talking. Within an instant he is on top of her, he strangles her, within an instant she is dead. . . . He's in a cocaine frenzy. . . . What was his intent? Listen to the evidence with a fair and open mind to see if this was premeditated or killing in a rage, without intent.

—Marc Carlos, *for the defense*

By the time *People v. English-Howard* was finally assigned to Judge William Kennedy in San Diego Superior Court in the summer weeks of late July 1995, I had gotten used to regular conversations with Peter Gallagher, the attorney for the prosecution. We were on a first-name basis. He was "Peter," and I was "Professor." We had been involved for almost a year in trial preparation. I had provided leads to resources for the case by helping him locate students and others at the university who could tell stories about Andrea's life, and by finding things that could evidence Andrea's political activities.

The first time I met Peter was a few days after the arrest of Andrés. He came to my campus office to talk to me and to meet some of the folks at the Women's Resource Center, and in the department, who knew Andrea as an activist.

"Hey, Professor, need to ask you a few questions."

Peter was an amiable, muscular Irishman with a sparkling, more than slightly acerbic wit. Although he was younger than I was, he was thick-skinned from years of working on the sexual abuse and domestic violence unit in the district attorney's office in San Diego. Homicide cases like this one were routine. Too routine, he said. More than anything, he wanted to be home, playing with his little girl, and helping his wife get back on track and finish her dissertation.

"After this case, that's it, I'm cutting back. Going to half time, at least until Eloise's finished with her writing. I'm tired of dealing with all these crooks." "Crooks" was his not-so-endearing term for all felony arrestees, regardless of offense.

Peter was dedicated to this case. He was smart. He wanted to win. Yet something else was pushing him. Andrea had gotten to him. He was becoming part of Andrea's extended family. He even came to the memorial service. Later, we would find ourselves visiting or calling Lesley within days of each other. "Say hello to Peter when you see him again," I would say. "How's the Professor?" he would ask.

On the Monday after the memorial service, a disturbing story appeared in the *Daily Aztec,* the student newspaper. William Beall, an enterprising young journalism student at SDSU, had gone to the city jail and interviewed English-Howard while he was awaiting arraignment. "Everyone's gonna make you out to be a monster," Beall had said to him. And then English-Howard denied he had anything to do with Andrea's murder.

"I have no idea what happened to her. I had nothing to do with her death," English-Howard had said. "There's no way in hell I'd ever raise my hand to her. . . . We were a team. . . . She was my future wife. . . . With the climate out there for a black man and a white woman, they're looking for someone to hang."

"What do you think about that?" I asked Peter. "Andrés says that he had nothing to do with killing Andrea. He said Lesley lied, out of stress, about the conversation with him. He says he never confessed, never told her he killed Andrea."

"Oh, Christ, the crook's whining. He's trying to turn it into a race thing. Pull an O. J. There's evidence all over the place. He did it. He's scared."

Later, at the trial, Beall would testify about his conversation with English-Howard. "I asked him what happened," Beall said, "and Andrés said that he'd come home, 'still a little buzzed,' the night of the murder, and 'found her ass there.' He said he knew that he would be blamed. So he ran." But, by then, English-Howard had confessed, and so the prosecution used this invented tale as yet another example of English-Howard's manipulation, of his lying to get attention. He'll say anything to get what he wants, they said.

Still, the story threw me into a loopy mood the day it was published. Could it be true? Andrés had talked about a missing key to their apartment. Someone else could have broken in. "Another dude did it." Well, that's possible, I thought. How could I be so sure that Andrés was the murderer? There had been no trial, yet, not even an arraignment. I knew enough about courts and cops and discrimination in San Diego to know that being a black man—well, I knew too much, both about what had happened and what might have happened.

What Andrés had said was not implausible. If you wanted implausible watch the O. J. trial, I thought. But wait, even there, same thing, I guess. No witnesses. Police could plant evidence. Batterers weren't necessarily murderers. And here we were, all of us, thinking back to our last times with Andrea, to the times we had seen her with him, well, really, we had seen nothing, nothing that anyone had seen was wrong. No history of abuse. No 911 calls to the police. And worse, Andrés was not O. J. There would be no dream-team attorneys, there were no quick trips to Chicago on fast jets, flying first class, chatting calmly with the flight attendants. No, Andrés had taken the bus to his mother's in Santa Cruz, stopping along the way, it later turned out, to make a few trips for cash to the ATM machine with his dead girlfriend's bank card. Well, bad judgment. Scared. Innocent until proven guilty. I had to teach a class. I'd better bring the psychologist.

Even after everything was over, after he was dead, I couldn't stop thinking about what Andrés had said in that interview: "They're looking for someone to hang." Who's "they?" I wondered.

I liked Peter a lot. He had a wonderful sense of outrage leavened with fistfuls of irony. I could always hear the person below the brash surface of the attorney. He became annoyed when several of the potential jurors that he had been most interested in securing had removed themselves from the panel because, they said, their working in a battered women's shelter meant they couldn't be neutral. He was dumbfounded by their utter lack of cunning.

"I don't get it. Why don't those who are experts on women's issues see themselves as expert and not as 'biased'? Why are only those who are part of the status quo, the dominant view, allowed to portray themselves as 'neutral'? Another woman eliminated herself today because she was a 'survivor.' I don't get it. I say, let all the experts be experts."

Even when he said he wanted a judge who wouldn't take too long impaneling a jury, even when he told me that he would abandon all sense of what he called "being PC" while he was constituting a jury—"I want a jury that will convict"—I still liked him. And when he called the defense's psychiatrist a "prostitute," I laughed it off. Prosecutor talk. Because, after all, he'd say all these outrageous things and then he'd remind me to phone

Lesley. "Yesterday was Andrea's birthday. Be sure to call Lesley. It's been a rough time for her." But he couldn't muster quite the same compassion for Andrés.

The day he called to tell me that Andrés had hung himself in prison, I was at a meeting. So he left the message on my answering machine at work.

"Hey Professor, I need to let you know . . . listen, English-Howard's dead. He hung himself. Call me."———

I was stunned. At the time, I thought it was bizarre, cold, almost cruel for him to leave that message. Only later did I realize that to have heard about Andrés from Peter was to have heard the news, even as awful as the recorded words were, from someone loving, someone who knew, who got it. Well, he got most of it. He didn't seem to understand my grief over this second death, over Andrés's death. Why wasn't I relieved, happy even, that it had ended this way? It was better that way, he told me, easier on everyone. But that was the palpable gap between us. You had to respect it. Because I could never understand how he kept himself balanced.

"This is a murder trial, folks. Cold-blooded murder. . . . What was his intent?"

We each had our jobs to do, didn't we?

"Say, listen, Professor, we got this thing pretty tight, but, I was wondering, can you find me that tape you told me about? You know, the one where Andrea is being interviewed about the Women's Resource Center."

"Sure."

"And say, what about any papers of hers? Anything that might say that she was intending to leave for San Francisco, anything that would show her deciding to leave, say, around October or so?"

"You know, I'm not sure what there is. But I have a paper from one of the students. One of the young women who was working with her in the center. Maybe there's something there."

So I dug through my files, and there it was: "Andrea will be leaving at the end of the semester."

"Bingo. Beautiful. Can I have a copy?"

"You can have the original. Here, let me make a copy. We need to keep all these records for the students' files."

Later in the month, as the investigation progressed, it became clear that the students knew a lot more about Andrea, about her life and what she had wanted to do, than any of us had realized, including the students themselves. They started calling the office, asking for advice, what to say, whom to talk to, whom to avoid. They had their stories. They felt burdened and scared by the stories. "I can't help but think. . . . I need to tell you. . . . I wish I had said. . . . I told her. . . . She was crying. . . . She was so strong." So they began to share these pieced-together stories of a life with one another.

And the many chords slowly strung themselves into a hauntingly atonal mythology that the students chanted like some rite of passage. With memory's songs they created a dirge, a prayer for all women's souls, which they intoned almost unthinkingly in order to get themselves out of what was surely the irrevocable, but not yet buried, past and into what was just as surely the possible, but not yet imaginable, next day. Most of the students never imagined that in the trial these psalms might become "evidence."

"You know, I'm getting worried about what will happen at the trial," I said one day to Polly. "Everyone keeps talking, and I am worried about whether anyone realizes that they might be subpoenaed, that they might have to testify. Do you think we should have a meeting to explain—I don't know—to explain what a criminal trial involves, what testimony is?"

"That might be a good idea."

We invited Michele Hagan, a lawyer who had worked in the city attorney's domestic violence unit, to a meeting organized for the students and asked her to explain the judicial process.

I had met Michele a few months before, at the same exhibit of Donna Ferrato's searing photographs of battered women, *Living with the Enemy,* that Andrea had attended only days before she died. Michele and I met at the exhibit's opening. Ferrato and Stacey Kabat, the producer of the Academy Award–winning film, *Defending Our Lives,* a documentary on battered women who had killed their attackers, were being feted at a ritzy reception in the lobby of the Lyceum Theatre in downtown San Diego. It was a benefit for the county's battered women's shelters and hot-line services for victims.

Everyone was politely circling the pictures, sipping wine, trying not to look too closely at the anguish in that woman's eyes, or to stare too long or too carefully at the shadow cast on that cowering woman's face by her husband's raised arm frozen in midswing near the edge of the frame, just off-center in the photographer's lens. I wondered if we were each thinking about the might have beens and weres of our own lives, silently comparing notes about whether it was as bad as it looked, as we remembered. Well, that was art for you. Made things look awful, but beautiful in their awfulness. It made me think.

"Hey, nice to meet you, finally," Michele said when a mutual friend came up to introduce us. "I've been wanting to talk with you about possibly coming to State to give some guest lectures. I'm not teaching now, got a business training attorneys in trial skills, but I like to teach and it would be good to stay in form."

Michele had worked for years in the San Diego city attorney's office, prosecuting cases against domestic violence offenders. She was an outspoken, tough-minded firebrand in the local world of attorneys. Chic, smart, full of humor, life, and principle, and unused to taking no for an answer, Michele found herself, a couple of years later, against the advice of just about all her friends and colleagues, stepping forward to be the witness in a suit filed against the city attorney's office. Initiated by Hagan's coworker, another female prosecutor, the suit had brought sexual harassment and discrimination allegations against both Hagan's former boss, Casey Gwinn, then the head of the domestic violence unit in the city attorney's office, and Gwinn's former superior, John Witt, who was the city attorney at the time of the events.

Gwinn is a prominent figure in the domestic violence arena. As one of the founding members of the influential San Diego Domestic Violence Council, he built his political career on the rightly touted legacy of his legal innovations. Gwinn helped develop precedent-setting arrest policies and aggressive domestic violence prosecution in San Diego, policies that meant that his office would not hesitate to bring cases to prosecution even without the victim's testimony. At the time of the suit, Gwinn was president of the Domestic Violence Council. He wasn't someone who wanted to find himself in a position that might embarrass him in the women's community. He wouldn't take it quietly.

That was exactly why Michele's testifying at the trial, and some of her comments being quoted in the press, must have pushed his buttons so hard. The jury returned a mixed verdict: It found that the female prosecutor had been wrongfully terminated and had been retaliated against when she complained to the city's equal employment opportunity commission. But it was divided on the discrimination issue. It isn't often that a jury has the courage to hold its public officials, especially the highly popular ones, accountable for their actions, making them personally liable and making them feel the pain in their own pocketbooks. Once the jury decided the case, the city council voted to foot the bill for damages assigned, under the provisions for broad protection from personal liability given to city officials acting in the capacity of their office.

Still, even if it didn't look so good for Gwinn, with his reputation as an unequivocally sympathetic advocate for women's rights, to be questioned in public, he had many defenders. He soon shook off the bad vibes. He survived, virtually unscathed. The case faded from the spotlight. Michele moved on.

"Well, sure, give me your card, and I'll let you know," I said to Michele. "Right now we have all our courses staffed, but a special lecture might be possible to arrange."

"Great, call me if you need me."

I did.

When Michele arrived on campus for the meeting with the students, I was still busy rounding them up. They weren't exactly eager to be found. But I felt they needed this reality check. I wanted them to hear what Michele had to say so that they could decide for themselves what they wanted to do. It was an odd lesson to be planning, but, I thought, a necessary one. I wanted to be sure that what we were doing with this informational meeting was not prejudicial in any legal sense. Michele assured me that she would stick to an outline of the legal process and stay away from any implications about what anyone should do or say.

She began a simple lecture, one you might hear in a class on the law for nonlawyers. She explained the basics of what a criminal trial might entail, she defined legal terms, she talked about how anyone ought to think about herself as a witness, if she chose to testify, and about what the rights of witnesses were.

Everyone sat quietly around the seminar table, apparently listening intently. Then Michele asked if there were any questions. No one said a word. They fidgeted in their seats, stared into space, seemed affectless. Michele waited. One by one, they started to pose the most oblique, tentative what ifs that must have made everyone in the room shiver at the cold reality of what we could hear, what lay beneath the surface innocence. Their hesitation told us what they really knew, or felt that they really knew, about what had happened.

I saw then for the first time that the students would be carrying the weight of this around with them a long, long time. Even if they decided never to talk to the defense, which they had the right to do, or avoided having to testify, which they could do unless they were subpoenaed, they were acting like witnesses to a crime. No, none of them had seen the murder. None of them had seen the accused fleeing the scene of the crime. None of them had heard any sounds of danger anywhere close to the exact time of Andrea's death. It wasn't that. They acted as if they had witnessed the slow, steady dissolution of a life, an erosion of strength that all the theories and all the intervention strategies known to their young feminist selves hadn't been able to prevent. Words had failed them; ideas had been no stronger allies.

The crime they had witnessed was that they had not been able to stop her dying. Now they were left behind to ponder the question that is every witness's fate to wonder about forever: Was there something else I could have done?

In the years following the trial, I would see these young women on the campus. Until they graduated and left what seemed to them like the scene of a crime, they had a kind of wounded look about them. You wouldn't have noticed it. They moved from one event to another easily enough, planning this or that rally, printing this or that flyer, studying for exams. But there was an edge, a too intense giggle, a chill in the air every fall.

Every anniversary of Andrea's death, at the annual Take-Back-the-Night rally and musical event that commemorates her murder, even if not on the exact day of it, we assemble on the steps of the free-speech area. If you look closely in the shadows cast by the candlelight, you can see the shawled ghosts on the edge of the crowd. Almost imperceptibly, I shudder at the sight of them. Their names are floating in the breeze on T-shirts hanging on clotheslines. Their lives have been memorialized in brief biographies of their intense deaths embossed on the bronze plaques attached to stately red silhouetted cutouts. These wooden, life-sized figures stand like silent witnesses to quite ordinary domestic dramas.

It was an unnerving hour.

"There's a lot of knowledge in that room," Michele said. "Tell anyone who needs to talk more that she can call me."

"Thanks. I will."

In those late spring months of 1994, I became an emissary, a courier between two worlds—the university and the court system. I couldn't tell which one made me feel more like I'd forgotten the basic definitions of words like truth, fairness, commitment. Truth kept getting mixed up with anger, or sometimes "right to fair trial," and then truth became evidence. Fairness contemplated commitment and gave testimony. "Well I'm sure she must have meant, . . ." or "Didn't you hear her say that? . . ." or "He was only pretending."

Like an emissary between two worlds, the ivory tower and the hall of justice. I know why it's a tower, but why is it ivory? Is it because there we find knowledge pure as the driven snow? Knowledge driven like the snow into the streets turns slushy grey under the traffic of human feet. And what about the hall of justice? Lives in the balance, justice takes a break and goes to a party. Her slip is showing. I was losing my bearings. I was losing my mother tongue.

But I had decided that I wasn't going to testify. I couldn't. I knew even then that I wanted to write about Andrea. Later. And because of that, I felt some strange attachment to what I called "being objective." Even though I had argued for at least a dozen years about the concept's ideological origins, objectivity was something that I now desired more than anything. I wanted to assume a place outside and above what was going on. I needed to assume that such a place existed. And I found it. But it wasn't where or what it was supposed to be.

Since I knew that objectivity was an achievement, I doubted the assertion that distance was something you could readily assume if you wanted to be fair. I knew that I would have to work at achieving objectivity. But I thought if I stayed out of the trial as a direct participant, if I sat in the gallery watching, I could call myself objective. "No, I didn't testify. I watched." If being objective was turning things that you cared about deeply into mere events that you could watch, I guess I never doubted that it was possible to achieve objective distance. I only worried that it would make me feel less human.

Then I thought about Hannah Arendt sitting in Eichmann's trial at Nuremburg. I thought about Arendt not because I saw any analogy between Eichmann and English-Howard, or because I thought their deeds were in any way similar. Far from it. Eichmann perpetrated unspeakable acts that caused immeasurable suffering to millions, and he never repented a single one of them. I thought about Arendt because I realized that she had been watching too. She had been watching something that was deeply connected to her life. And she must have been implicated in what she watched. I wondered how she had felt about watching.

Sitting in the audience at the Jerusalem trial, Arendt wrote in *Eichmann in Jerusalem,* were "survivors" like herself, who "knew by heart all there was to know, and who were in no mood to learn any lessons and certainly did not need this trial to draw their own conclusions. As witness followed witness and horror was piled upon horror, they sat there and listened in public to stories they would hardly have been able to endure in private, when they would have had to face the storyteller." The more the prosecution's rhetoric brought the larger issues, the horror of the Holocaust itself, into focus, the more the accused, the man, Eichmann, receded into the background. What Arendt meant by all this was that the more the trial put into its center the social system of Nazism and anti-Semitism, the less the man Eichmann seemed to be responsible for what had happened.

A criminal trial must, Arendt observed, keep at its center the doer, not the horror of the deeds. The doer must be held accountable for what he has done, for the crime of what he has done.

Maybe I watched simply to protect myself from having to take the witness stand. I didn't know how much watching would cost.

"You know, I don't really need you to testify," Peter told me early on. "I mean, you'd be credible, you'd be a strong witness, but I think I have a good enough case without you. So, no, Professor, I don't need you to testify."

"Are you sure?"

"Yeah, I'm sure. You can help me just as much without taking the stand. Maybe more."

So much for achieved distance.

Watching cost me a lot. It's hard to define, but watching cost me the ability to take sides easily. All the years of feminist theory had convinced me that the position of a distanced observer was an ethical dead end. I mean, I thought that if you really got "outside" an event, then you would never understand what was happening "inside." I believed that you needed to take up the position of the other, that you needed to imagine yourself to be the one you thought you would never be. Then, from the inside, you might understand that the darker (what a metaphor!) side of human existence was still a part of human existence. I believed you could only understand "the other" by lessening the distance between you and him. You needed to get close to the "evil" that you thought you were only observing. And you could only get there through empathy or a perceived, shared identification with the marginal, the outsider, the outcast, the outlaw. But watching taught me that it's more complicated than that.

Arendt saw something much more terrifying because she watched. Arendt's watching allowed her to see that the horror of Eichmann was that he was not a "monster" at all. He was as utterly normal as the rest of the world in which he was immersed. The horror of Eichmann was that he was completely incapable of thinking, that is, he could not think from the standpoint of somebody else. Arendt said that the horror of Eichmann was that he showed us the "banality of evil," the terrifying normality of his complete inability to tell right from wrong. Because she watched, she was prevented from taking sides. And that enabled her to see that Eichmann's lack of any motive except his own "extraordinary diligence"—his inability to see something, anything, from the point of view of anybody else—was what made him, because of his remoteness from reality, capable of "wreak[ing] more havoc than all the evil instincts taken together."

But for me, watching did not bring me face to face with any kind of evil. Watching brought me into close range with someone who was immensely confused, but not thoughtless. I saw that the second day of the trial, when Andrés stood up and turned to face all of us, all of us who had watched the back of his head, or his ears, or his hands scribbling notes to his attorneys.

He rose as the judge called recess, just as he had the first day. But then, slowly, unexpectedly, he turned to face the courtroom semifilled with spectators, mostly friends and family of Andrea. He stood still for a long moment, his handcuffed hands folded over one another, staring, silently. For the first time I saw that he was a handsome man. His mustachioed, full face was somber now and he had the buff frame of a bodybuilder who hadn't overdone it, had kept a sense of balance in his body work. That's odd, I thought. Balance. Limits. Boundaries. Control. His crisp white shirt gave him the awkward appearance of someone dressed for a job interview who had forgotten his suit jacket and is trying to look inconspicuous in a room where he is slowly beginning to realize that he doesn't belong. I felt that he was waiting for someone to see him. I had to fight back the strong urge to call out his name.

"Look at that. He's giving me the creeps, looking at us," Polly said to me while we were filing out of the row to go to lunch. It made me feel un-comfortable too. But it wasn't until months later, when I was looking at pictures of Andrés that Andrea had sent her mom about a year earlier, pictures of the two of them cuddling, or of Andrés with a silly grin on his face, playing with the dog, that I began to understand that something else had happened in that moment in the courtroom when he stared at us all. He wasn't in a glass bubble, he was before us all, a man, admitting what he had done.

When I was watching at the trial, watching Andrés, watching Andrea's family and friends, I found that I had to pay attention. And that was the first step toward caring about all those people I was watching. While I was watching, I found that I existed not so much either on the outside or on the inside, but in a kind of suspended zone, a "zone of attention." And when I was in that place, in that moment, I wasn't exactly empty of thought, or without my own concerns. I was open, vulnerable, available for interaction. I was listening hard, paying attention, watching.

So, no, I don't think that I identified either with Andrea or with Andrés. I found that I thought about them both in terms of relationships—in terms of friends, mothers, daughters, sons. Even if your friend or your daughter or your mother or your son did something really stupid, even really horrible, what would it mean for you to hate them, I wondered? What would that hate enable you to feel or to *do*? The only thing that it would give you access to was the same kind of rage or vengeful action that you hated them for practicing—either a self-hatred or a fury forced on another. Maybe you'd wish you or they were dead. It was much harder to imagine loving them for the stupid or hateful things that they did. What would that give you access to? What would that love enable you to feel, to *do*? Could you be a lover in the courtroom? That was why I found it hard to take sides.

While I was watching, I began to become aware of myself watching. Then, watching made me watch myself. Once you turn yourself into an object, you understand what's lost by watching. Innocence. Innocence is lost through watching. Turn something into an object and you lose your innocence.

I began to think again about the two portraits of Andrés, the killer, presented in the opening arguments. I began to think again about all the portraits of Andrea, the victim, that I had painted and had had painted for me over these months, now years. All those portraits became the same person seen from different angles. But every time I thought like this, watching had taken me out of the trial and into some other place, into a place beyond and after the trial.

In the criminal courtroom, no such ambiguity is permissible. Or rather, ambiguity raises the kinds of doubts, called reasonable, that are supposed to lead juries not to convict. Ambiguity is a disaster for the prosecution. Where is truth in the courtroom, then? It moves around. It takes sides. It's an ally of the suspicious, the gullible, the credulous, the bored. Truth snuggles up to the most rhetorically persuasive argument. It's an unfaithful companion of the sly. The creation of juries, truth's the coveted prize that will never belong to the bashful, or to the meek. It's the reward given to the most cunning legal strategies, whether prosecution or defense. Truth has no known natural sponsors. We're going to have to fight for the truth. That's why justice is blind. She can't stand the fray. I didn't know if I could be on truth's side.

Of course I wanted Andrés to be convicted. There was no alternative. He had killed Andrea. By the time of the trial, he had admitted that he killed her. He took drugs. He admitted that too. It took an effort of will and thought to wrap my mind around the legal concept of intent under those circumstances. I began to wonder about the difference between murder and wrongful death.

I also feared what would happen if Andrés was convicted. Here were many of us, witnesses, folks who said we knew that there was something wrong. But we did nothing. He alone would be held responsible for what happened. That was the only possible outcome of a criminal trial: He was either guilty or not. He alone would be in prison for a very long time. That, too, was the only possible outcome of the punishment that criminal guilt demands. He would be another black man in prison for a very long time. And all of us, we would still be here, outside, living. Would we be innocent if he was guilty?

People and things, fragments, the shadow traces of what was left of Andrea. The prosecution used these, our sketches, to create a portrait of Andrea's actions and thoughts in the days closest to her death and created a story about how these actions and thoughts made her lover, Andrés, want to kill her.

"When did she tell you she was going to leave?"

"Early October, she said she was going to San Francisco, she was training two other young women to take over the center. She said she wanted to go to San Francisco for political support. And, she was in a bad relationship; she needed to leave."

"She said she was scared about his using drugs. She knew she had to go."

"Did she plan to leave?"

"Yes. She loved him, she didn't want to hurt him, dump him."

"Did she have a plan?"

"She was making arrangements . . ."

"Early in October I told Andrea that I had been having problems. She said, 'It can't be as bad as mine.' I knew she had been keeping her clothes at the Women's Resource Center since September. I saw her clothes there. She slept on the couch. She had a blanket and a pillow. We were at Monty's on November 3, having lunch. She was stressed, crying. She said that Andrés had threatened suicide, she was watching him twenty-four hours to make sure he didn't do it."

"Was she afraid of Andrés?"

"Not physically, only emotionally. She was a role model, she was afraid that if they [the other women at the center] knew about her problems at home, that they wouldn't respect her or look up to her anymore."

"Did she defend him when you confronted her with the question, Why not leave?"

"She was defending her own decision."

"So, you knew where the shelters were. You'd think that she knew. She had this great fear and you told her to deal with it next week?"

"Yes [in tears], I gave her bad advice."

One student's report about working at a field placement in the Women's Resource Center under Andrea's direction helped the prosecution define intent in this case. Many women who are in abusive relationships, whether physically dangerous or not, experience the greatest threat to their safety from manipulative or controlling partners at precisely the time that they decide to leave. Andrea's very public announcement of her forthcoming move, recorded in this student's report as the student's concern about the future of the center without Andrea, became evidence that the prosecution used to establish how threatened Andrés felt when he began to realize that the relationship that he had depended upon was ending. First he tried a phony suicide attempt, the prosecution said; then he decided to kill her.

"I just wanted to make her shut up," Andrés said at the trial.

"And you sure did that," Peter countered.

Other students testified that Andrea had confided in them about having problems at home. On November 3, 1994, Andrea had lunch with Corinne and Joy, two women who worked with her at the center, both women's studies majors. The three talked for about an hour and a half about all sorts of stuff. Then the conversation got personal. Andrea started to cry. One of the women said, "Have you started to lie about your boyfriend to your friends?" Andrea told them about Andrés's suicide attempts. She was scared. She was trying to help him. She put him on her own personal twenty-four-hour suicide watch. "She knew he was afraid of her leaving; she said he was afraid of her leaving."

"And yet with all these signs, with all this warning, you didn't have any problems driving her home that night, leaving her there with her boyfriend, with whom she was fighting?" The defense was trying to unsettle the prosecution's witness.

Lost innocence. Maybe I said I'd watch just to protect myself from taking the witness stand, from standing in public and telling what I knew.

I knew about the lines that we draw between ourselves and the world. We must be professionals. If we want to maintain credibility, we have to keep our distance. What we talk about in the classroom and what happens in the world, these are very distinct things. We draw the line. We say we can't get too involved. We have to be careful. We must take care of ourselves. But at the same time, we find caring difficult and comfort hard to come by.

Lost innocence, perhaps. Thinking back on all these events, we hesitate the next time in class before we describe, before we interpret, before we settle in our theories what's happening in a situation. Perhaps we wonder about the sides that we have taken. Perhaps we introduce more ambiguity into a setting, encourage more critical inquiry into a problem, continue more diligently to subject our assumptions to reevaluation. Maybe we offer examples of difficult ordinary situations in which women and men find themselves where the lines of oppression and resistance are not so clearcut. When we interpret any event, in the classroom—whether it is a rape reported in the press, a law for gender equality that has been defeated, or gains made by women in the workforce—maybe we think, can we be so sure our interpretation is right? Watching, from the outside.

David Ohten was an athletic coach at SDSU, the strengthening and conditioning coach for the Aztec athletes. In fall 1993 he met Andrea and took an instant liking to her. She was fit, she worked out, she wanted a job as a student assistant in the weight room. David hired her and, later, when Andrea wanted to pursue advanced self-defense training, he trained her himself.

"She asked me to let Andrés work out in the weight room, too. I said sure. Then, later, in the fall, I saw that she was not the same, she was upset. She came to talk to me on three different occasions about her personal life."

I'm thinking, this is interesting: women's studies student seeks weight coach's advice on how to deal with difficult interpersonal life. Well, of course, why not? He knew about athletes. He knew about jocks and their habits. She asked David to help her find a drug counselor for Andrés. Could she have asked any of us that?

"Then, in late October, she came to see me again, to talk," David said. "She was upset, looked like she'd been crying. She said Andrés had taken money from her. I asked her if he hit her. She said no. I offered to let her stay at my house, with my wife and me. She said she'd think about it."

"Did she know self-defense?"

"Oh, yes."

"Could she escape from a choke hold?"

"Yes."

"From the front?"

"Yes. She was a natural."

"What do you mean by that, a 'natural'?"

"Well, I mean, she could just do it, not think, just react. I taught her moves from behind, how to get out of rear choke holds. Normally, you would pass out in five to ten minutes, so you go for the nerve point in the hand. She was learning how to strike and kick. She was versed. I used to surprise her when I'd see her on campus. I'd try to catch her off guard. She was good."

I think, how do you prepare yourself for a choke hold from someone you love?

I am watching a tape of Andrea, a tape of her practicing her self-defense routines. She is in the SDSU gym. You can tell that she is proud and a little nervous to be having herself taped. She runs up eagerly, but shyly, to the camera and says her name. "Andrea O'Donnell." "Say it louder," someone says in the background. So she runs up to the camera again and announces herself more loudly, assertively. "Demonstration tape," she says. She lines up in front of a dozen or so guys, each of whom comes at her in an un-expected way, each of whom is differently sized, differently shaped. She decks them all, without fail. She moves to increasingly complex tricks, falls, holds. She flips them, she makes them trip, she gets them to the ground, they are disarmed. Then the teacher asks her to assume a prone position. On her back, she fends off the would-be intruder, makes him get off her. She flips him over. Again and again. I play the tape in slow motion. Slowly, his hands reach for her neck. Slowly, she breaks his hold.

Slowly, Andrés grabs her. She tells him he is hurting her. She calls for the dog.

Without Blame

If you had been reading the *New York Times* with any degree of scru-tiny on April 26, 1975, you might have noticed a tiny article in the Metro-politan Briefs headlined, "A Mother and Her Child."

> A State Supreme Court justice ruled that although the mother of a 6-year-old boy was living with her lover and her child and could hardly be designated for a 'mother of the year' award, her style of life did not make her unfit to retain custody of the child. Justice Louis B. Heller of Brooklyn declared that 'residence together of an unmarried male and female without the benefit of a sermonized marriage is not per se evil or immoral.'
>
> The names of the couple were not disclosed.

There have been many times over the last twenty years or so that I have thought about Judge Louis B. Heller's court in Brooklyn and the weeks that I spent there in the winter of 1975. I have wondered not so much about the finer points of justice as how I ever wound up in that courtroom in the first place. And how I ever got out alive. Not that my life was directly on the line. But I believed, and still do with all my heart, that if my son had been taken from me I would have been unable to live.

I can still feel the intense fright that came over me whenever I let myself imagine that I might be judged unfit, that I might lose my son. You know the feeling. Like the times you've been driving in a sort of daydream and you notice at the very last second that the driver of car ahead of you has suddenly slammed on the brakes. You're breathless. Then the adrenaline kicks in and a wave of pure heat rushes over you. It's your own heart pounding, beating out the realization that life can be gone in an instant.

How do I retrace the steps that I must have taken to stand before the judge and defend my maternal instincts? How do I explain how I got to that place where my mothering was called into question, where my own son, Jed, was no longer only the one I loved unconditionally and always, protected from danger all day and every night, but an object for judicial and psychological inspection? How did I decide to walk into that zone where my entire family, or at least the members of it who were still in my life, were transformed into character witnesses, and where a legion of my friends prepared to talk about me in court? I guess I have to begin before the wedding.

If I go back to that time before the wedding, I remember passion, excitement, energy, friendship, struggle. I am glad that I can recover that "before." It has been a life support system that has helped me breathe more than once in my life. I wouldn't want to lose "before."

After the case, years after, when Jed had moved back to New York to be with his father, when he chose to do that because his father and I had, luckily, both regained our senses, just in time to rediscover some small part of the love that we must have felt for one another, that life support system proved a handy invention. With it, we caught a whiff of "before." With it, we were able to exhale our embattled hostilities and the competition that had built walls between us and breathe in and near one another again so that we could make Jed, and our mutual love of Jed, the center of our now-dissolved family.

Our breathing in each other's company helped Jed see that he had a choice. It wasn't a choice between whom to love, we told him, just about where to live. It was only a choice between New York and California. We told him that he could choose where to live, but that we would never ask him (again) to choose which of us to love more. I only wish that we had added one more sentence. "And please forgive us, Jed, for ever having asked you to do that before."

Because of that life support system, I have lived to this time "after." Here, after, I have little anger any more for what happened during. But I have to go back to the time before to get to the time after. Then I can show you the not so simple arc that took me into court in 1975 and out and beyond and into another court, twenty years later, merely as an observer.

I was married when I was eighteen. It sounds better, I guess, to say that by then I had finished my first year of college. But not much better. I am surprised that we got married at all. Both of us had our doubts, at different times. He, so he said, because of the war, the possibility of being drafted. I, so I said, because of college, the possibility of all the freedom that I saw around me in 1966, even in the Bronx. I was at Fordham University then, at Thomas More College, the women's college, because Fordham was still only for men. He was teaching, working on his doctorate. I told him he could get a conscientious-objector exemption from the draft—he was studying comparative religion, after all. He told me I could keep my promises. We each did what we were told.

There I am in my white dress, not exactly a virgin. There he is in his tuxedo. He's not exactly a virgin either. We are in the chapel of the convent of nuns who taught me in high school. They loved our storybook romance. We were such a perfect couple. He, the clever, young debate coach, me, the even younger star debater. And, look, there's Brian, the best man. We used to play bridge with Brian and his mother. He lived with his mother until he was twenty-eight. I hated bridge. I couldn't keep the sets in my head. I'd rather think about other things. Brian says to John to stop complaining. Not everyone is good at bridge. A few years later Brian is dead. Died smoking in bed, asleep from the booze, I think. Hey, wow, there's Terry, my maid of honor, my high school debate partner, my college roommate. She's wearing that awful yellow dress with the green velvet bows and her hair is stuck up high on her head. Why are we all so stiff? We are too stiff for 1967.

I turn and there's my grandfather leaning over to give me a kiss. He is so happy, but he wishes my grandmother were there to see me. "Och, Kathleen," he says, "you look so grand. I wish she were here to see you."

And then he starts to cry. My mother isn't there, thank god. She's outside, I think, or maybe at the bar on the corner. My father isn't there. He's outside. But nowhere near my mother. He's not very happy about any of this at all. "You wouldn't listen," he says.

I don't think I had any imagination when it came to marriage. I mean, I didn't imagine that it would be anything in particular. My parents' marriage had rid me forever of the idea of calm and comfort and marital bliss. And I never believed the portraits of connubial splendor in women's magazines. I wasn't much of a fan of those. I was both too Catholic and too much more interested in *Newsweek, Time, Keating's Contemporary Archives,* and all the other chronicles of world events that champion high school debaters learn to covet more than *Glamour* or *Cosmopolitan.* But if I didn't have an imagination when it came to marriage, I did at least hope for predictability.

John did too. He predicted a wife. So I went to cooking school—Anna Szekeley's School of Cooking on the Upper East Side of Manhattan. I enjoyed the long subway ride from Flatbush Avenue to Seventy-Seventh Street as much as I did being the youngest misfit among a gaggle of upper-middle-class, genuine full-time housewives who were all preparing, I assumed, for a lifetime of serving Hungarian goulash to a select party of eight. I tried to imagine dinner parties in my small Brooklyn apartment on Nostrand Avenue. With or without Hungarian paprika, it didn't feel the same. At least those women were living in Manhattan and not Westchester. I'd give them that. I hadn't read Betty Friedan or John Cheever for nothing. While I was learning the fine art of béarnaise one day, I remember thinking, here is one way I will not be like my mother. The best part was that we got to eat what we cooked.

I predicted a husband. So John provided material comfort and conformed to his expectations of his role. To mine too, mostly, I suppose. But my ideas were changing too fast. I wanted more. More of his time than he was able to give. More companionship. More . . . friendship. He didn't understand what I needed. I hardly really understood it myself. He knows that now; we both do.

The year before we got married, a year before Andrea was born, I discovered existentialism, Simon and Garfunkle, and Rimbaud. I learned about Rimbaud from my good friend Sharon Connare. I had met Sharon during my first days at Fordham. She was one of the wittiest, zaniest, smartest, most "sixties" people I knew. When I didn't stay at my own apartment on Decatur Avenue, because my roommate, Terry, had her boyfriend over, or because I wanted a change of scenery, Sharon and I spent silly nights at her boardinghouse room, reading French symbolist poetry, giggling, talking about Kierkegaard, and debating the Vietnam War, while we waited for the chemicals to straighten my hair.

We stank the house up with all that stuff—the poetry, the existentialism, the radical politics, and the hair straightening—so much that Sharon's landlady refused to renew her lease. Sharon didn't care. She was moving to Bensalem, the new experimental college that Fordham had just established, she told me. It was going to be a genuine commune, with an egalitarian cadre of faculty and students handpicked for their ability to contribute to and thrive in intense interdisciplinary seminars and relationships freed from power. They would share living quarters in an apartment building donated to the university, build a nonhierarchical learning environment, and bring on the revolution.

To me, Bensalem represented the sixties. I dreamed about the great commune movements of the 1840s in America. When I visited the unimposing red brick building any time that next year, I could easily imagine the ghosts of Fanny Wright and Robert Owen wandering the halls of Bensalem, bumping into the likes of Jimi Hendrix, Allen Ginsberg, the Grateful Dead, the Living Theater, Gloria Steinem, Students for a Democratic Society, chanting together about the holy trinity of sex, drugs, and sixties rock 'n' roll. I was jealous. I missed Sharon. I was getting married.

Leaving Fordham in 1967, I transferred to Brooklyn College. No tuition and no subway ride for two hours from the basement of Brooklyn to the attic of the Bronx. John and I rented a small place in a newer apartment building only a few bus stops from the university. I had no trouble taking classes, doing the shopping, the cooking, the cleaning, the housewifely waiting for hubby to come home, all in one effortless routine. I felt like an anomaly, an anachronism. I felt lonely and old. I wanted to quit. John told me I should stay in school. So I did.

It turned out that Brooklyn College was an electrifying place for a young Catholic woman to find herself in the sixties. It had long been influenced by the strength of Jewish liberal intellectualism that was quite prominent throughout the New York City public university system. I soaked it up. Some of the most stunning professors in the world introduced me to John Updike, Martha Graham, Max Weber, Simone de Beauvoir, Arnold Schoenberg, the Dadaists, and the Chinese revolution. And being the odd person out, the marginalized Catholic in a world of Jews, taught me a lot about myself, about being a minority, about the politics of ethnicity and sexuality, about ghettoes. When our marriage was ending, John used to say that Brooklyn College ruined me. He may have been right. But at the time, I felt born again.

I had already started to dance again at Fordham. But at Brooklyn College in 1968, it was possible to imagine that Emma Goldman's revolutionary aesthetics was more than rhetoric. We studied with Jimmy Truitt, who had been a member of Alvin Ailey's company, and Paul Sanasardo and other Martha Graham aficionados.

I spent morning, noon, and night in the dance studio. When I wasn't in that studio in Brooklyn, I was taking a subway uptown to go to someone's Manhattan dance loft. I felt the smells and sights and rhythms of the antiwar movement, of the emerging women's movement and the sexual revolution all roll into one scintillating temptation that was New York City in 1968. "Remember why we are here," Sanasardo said one day, while we were in the studio and our friends were on the barricades outside, protesting the escalation of the Vietnam War, occupying the administration building to block the ROTC from campus. It was clear that we were being distracted from balancing at the barre. "We are *here* for a reason, not outside. Let it go, for now."

But the war wasn't something you could let go. Friends were being drafted, killed. Other friends were being beaten by the cops at protest marches that by now were an almost weekly occurrence. We gathered after rehearsal one night for a candlelight vigil in the old quad and listened in awe as the list of names of the newly dead took nearly four hours to read. I decided to major in dance and political science. An odd but appropriate combination—we were thinking about hearts and minds, you have to remember. "Meeting today, after class, to help organize the guerrilla theater group." Guerrilla theater to protest the guerrilla war.

Married, I dallied on the edges of dancing for the revolution until I was seven months pregnant and the *tondues* and *passés* became too difficult to perform with an off-center of gravity and a head full of confusion about what roles to play—erstwhile anarchosyndicalist or bohemian dropout mother or patient housewife or disillusioned Catholic or dutiful daughter.

I took my politics with me to the hospital the night that Jed was born. On the way to giving birth, with John driving and worrying nervously if we would make it all the way from Brooklyn to the hospital on the edge of Queens, I finished writing my final paper on the theory of surplus value in Marx. The professor was very understanding of the fact that I hadn't typed the paper. I got an A.

It was 1969, the year before *Our Bodies, Our Selves* was first published. Not much of the goings on in the Boston Women's Health Collective had filtered into my Brooklyn neighborhood. But somehow I got it into my head that I was going to have a "natural childbirth" and would nurse my baby. I even managed to find a class near the hospital where a nurse gave instructions on infant care and encouraged me to follow my instincts. In St. Joseph's Hospital where I gave birth, doctors were in charge of a New Testament approach to parturition. Lie on your back, feet up in the stirrups, doctor knows best. I couldn't push Jed out. Still half-drugged and stupefied, I awoke after the birth in such a state of oblivion that I thought the nurse was crazy when she told me I had had a son. I couldn't even remember being pregnant.

But I succeeded on the breast-feeding front. Since I was the only woman on the ward to nurse my child, there was no mistaking whose screaming infant got walked down the halls to whose swollen breasts in Room 209 every four hours, all through the night. Luckily my roommate was understanding. More than that, she was sad. She had never even thought about the option of breast-feeding, had never even imagined that it might be a kind of pleasure for her to hold her daughter close, so coupled with her own flesh that the milky, bloody moments between conception and birth would merge together, producing that sweetly curdled smell of timeless connections, an aroma so strong and distinctive that—even when it all ended, as it must—it left behind, on the surface of the skin, long years after the child had grown, the faint odor of that suckling. We cried together after she asked the doctor if she could change her mind, choose to nurse now that she had thought about it, only to hear him say, politely, firmly, yet a little impatiently, that the pills she had agreed to take within a few hours of the birth were already shriveling her mammary glands, already shrinking the possibilities. That was my first experience with consciousness raising. It hurt.

Jed was born in January. I spent the winter months pushing his baby carriage through the slushy streets of Brooklyn. I longed for friends my own age. Someone to confide my insecurities to. My neighbors in the building were mostly married women already working on their second or third child. College was a waste now, they said. I had a child. Surely I wouldn't think of sacrificing my maternal duties on the altar of my intellectual curiosity? I hadn't thought of it that way.

Cut off from the world I had known before, mortified at my own obvious failing in the face of Dr. Spock's *Baby and Child Care* standards, I felt I'd entered an order more cloistered than the Carmelites.

Sometimes, when I think about that time, and so many of the other girls in my high school, like me, who were already married, already had kids, I know that we were all desperate in our own ways. Desperate to be loved as we'd been promised. Desperate for an adult conversation. Desperate to know how to mother well enough. Desperate to learn the formula for mixing isolation with yearning into a brew not too potent for us to imbibe so young.

Eight months after Jed was born, I went back to school to finish my degree in political science. And to perform in the senior dance concert. When we had late rehearsals, I'd take Jed with me and he'd giggle on my hip, or fall asleep on a cushion stage left, while I practiced marking steps to Vivaldi, never thinking twice that the theater was not a normal place for a toddler to be with his mother, especially after midnight. He was so happy there, and I was happy with him there. He loved all the people, and they all loved him right back. I like to think, now, that those smells and sounds from the theater seeped into Jed's brain so deeply that it partly explains my actor son's love for the stage today.

I began to consider graduate school because some of my professors encouraged me to think that I was bright and I had the audacity to believe them. I really had no idea what I was doing. And something else, maybe the skeptical spirit of those protofeminist times, kept pushing me away from the predictability of traditional wifedom.

John considered the whole idea of graduate school ludicrous. We'd argue about it to the point of banality. "No wife of mine . . ." "You just don't understand me. You're never around." Then a friend recommended I read Shulamith Firestone's *Dialectics of Sex*. "I couldn't put it down," she said. "Especially the chapter on love." I hated the book when I first read it. But it had an undeniable impact; it hit too close to home. Years later, reading one of Andrea's student papers about her own struggles with issues of autonomy and connection in her relationship with Andres, I realized how little had changed from a generation earlier. We were both looking for some answer as if it was a message hidden in the back pages of a book.

So I squirreled away my birth control pills in the night table, had an affair or two not worth remembering, and still tried to be a good mother, tried to stay married and sane.

But my mother's death the next year triggered something in me, I think. I found myself putting money that I had inherited through her life insurance policy into a bank account in my own name. It was the first time, as an adult, that I had any money of my own. With this money marked by the pain of my mother's unlived life, I started graduate school over John's protests. Within a year, John and I had separated.

That summer I moved into a tiny apartment sublet in a Brooklyn Heights brownstone. I squeezed Jed's crib into the hallway between the single studio room and the bathroom and, in that cramped space, accepted all the responsibilities of single motherhood that I imagined were waiting for me. I felt more expansive and liberated than I had in years.

The roof from the flat below created a faux patio out my rear windows, overlooking a sultry, Manet-colored summer garden. On humid nights filled with crescendos of locusts screeching at the moon, when Jed was finally asleep, I'd climb onto the roof and catch the cool breezes blowing across the East River into Brooklyn. They banked down from the Promenade and swung up Henry Street, piquing my imagination with wild things outlined by the Manhattan skyline. Both freer and more alone, I was, I think, in a curious state of euphoria mixed with quiet terror when I met Mike.

It was hard to resist Mike's self-conscious mixture of indiscreet humor and bawdy intellectualism. Hard for me, anyway. The crazy way we walked across the Brooklyn Bridge talking all night on our first date should have warned me. Not that it would have mattered. I was willingly magnetized, drawn by my own desires to this man's conversation. Mesmerized by words that bespoke a poetic hedonism, a cavalier defiance of restraint, even, sometimes, an indignant ignorance of another's desire to respond as well as to listen, I gave in to the temptation of his speech. We fell in love.

Mike could talk for hours, laugh at his own jokes louder than anyone, and stare at strangers on the subway with such concentrated force that, more than once, I wanted to bolt. But even if I never understood what frightening ancient forces threatened to engulf him most of his waking hours, it didn't matter. And if there were no limits in time or space to his voluble passion, it didn't matter. That was the hook for me: I knew I could survive. I already had. Just like Andrea knew she could.

Mike's passionate needs and desires mixed with my own equally passionate ones and created a dynamic between us. They played all the chords I had learned to recognize from all the earliest symphonies of my life. Songs of disorder; the yearning, plaintive arias of the sick; the simple call to mitigate suffering but also the need to suffer myself so as to feel alive—this triumphant chorus of sad songs, mixed with the music of desire, until I felt an almost irresistible response. Almost, because I was sometimes the conductor. Almost, because I did not want the chorus to stop. It carried me on its somber, soothing, scintillating rhythms into a relationship and eventual marriage that was at once exciting and fulfilling and draining. Punctuated by bittersweet melodies, it lasted twelve years. It was in the earlier stages of this complex love for Mike that I nearly lost custody of my son Jed.

It all started so simply.

I was summoned to court as the defendant in a case brought by John to transfer custody of Jed from me to him. At the time, Jed was six. I was panicked at the thought of losing him.

"Don't worry. It's predictable," my attorney had said. "It's more for harassment value than anything. Since you sued him for increased child support, he's retaliated with this suit. It's no big deal."

"OK. But what do we have to do to move this quickly?" I asked, not so sure that there wasn't more to it than legal positioning.

"Well, that depends on how the judge reads the case, whether or not he thinks there's any real reason to consider this seriously." She was trying to allay my anxiety. "Let's see what the specifics are that he brings into court."

We won the suit for more child support and I was temporarily relieved. What could John possibly have to say that could make his suit a serious effort to take Jed from me? I hadn't done anything wrong. I loved Jed. He was thriving. I was the Rock of Gibraltar in Jed's life. And he in mine.

I had made sure that Jed's needs and Mike's needs didn't come into conflict too often. At least, I thought I had.

But, like Andrea, I was a survivor, schooled to care. Mike could spend hours a day immersed in his books, pondering the finer points of philosophy like some Talmudic scholar oblivious to the seasons of living. What danger was there in that? Even if he got a little edgy when Jed interrupted with the mellifluous noise of his clanging trucks or zoomed through the rooms with abandon, so what? I allowed us all to agree that I didn't need that kind of cushioned space to think; I could think anywhere, anytime, even interrupted constantly by Jed. We were just fine.

Yet with all this practiced survival I couldn't have prepared myself for the humiliation of being on trial. I never expected to have to defend myself, explain where I was and with whom and why, prove myself to be a good enough mother. I didn't consider what it would mean to my sense of dignity to have to turn my friends into witnesses and my son into a prize put before Solomon to assign. No, it wasn't a murder trial; I was only asked to prove that I wasn't endangering my son's life by my own.

John summoned the best devices to distinguish between good and bad mothers that the law had to offer—measure the generosity or parsimony of the mothering by the portrait of the child that can be captured through psychological tests.

Advised to retaliate with our own professionals, we submitted a counter-portrait of Jed. If anything, they said, Jed was distressed more by the contest between his parents in court than by anything else.

So John brought witnesses who could testify to my being insufficiently caring. They were people who knew me well, who remembered those times, so many years ago, when I was a young bride yet had behaved as if I never wanted to be a mother at all. Why, Sister Marguerite remembered how many times Kathy had hired her sister-in-law to baby-sit for Jed while she went to meetings or just went out, instead of caring for her son herself.

We retaliated with our own collections of friends and family. Transformed into witnesses, they set aside any conflicting observations or interpretations to describe a measured portrait of my life, casting me as innocent, mellowing Mike's moods.

We needed to be seen as an almost normal family, a tryptych that, save for what the court called "living together without benefit of clergy," would look like any other nice young couple and their son. In court, what really happens in a life matters less than how it can be portrayed.

We argued in court for three days, carping at one another, behaving dreadfully, finding whatever friends and family we could to drag each other down, to win, to win. It got so bad, the judge said, the picture we painted of Jed was so contradictory and our acrimony so intense that he had to meet Jed for himself to see which one of the "Jeds" was real.

I was stunned by the easy way that the most innocent things anyone might do—like staying up too late or loving too much—can be made to indicate a degree of moral torpor beyond repair. Judged unfit. Merely by someone's declaring it to be so. I began to believe it might be possible that I would lose my son. I even thought I might deserve it. After all, I hadn't thought enough about what Jed might be experiencing, in the middle of the tumult of my life. No, that wasn't really it. I had thought a lot about it. The truth was, I was afraid that I hadn't done enough to protect him. I was truly sorry. Nothing would ever be enough.

My father came to court every day. He said almost nothing while we ate our breakfast together at the same coffee shop each morning of the trial. He sat behind me in the courtroom and listened to the various experts and witnesses for the plaintiff who bandied about their wisdom in an effort to convince everyone of my incompetence.

To counter the words of Sister Marguerite, fingers fidgeting on her rosary (Hail Mary full of grace blessed be the fruit of thy womb), eyes assiduously heavenward whenever I would try to catch her glance, I gathered the testimony of my friends, agnostics every one. "Mike and Kathy are a wonderful couple, very loving, very normal. Jed is a very happy, adjusted child."

Through this my father sat and waited his turn.

On the next to the last day of the hearing, I watched my father walk down the aisle and take a seat to the left of the judge. He put his hand on the Bible and swore to tell the whole truth. Expressionless, he looked out through his thick glasses into the room at nothing in particular. He had his mind set on a task. He knew what he had to say.

"My name is Edward Jones and I am the grandfather of Jed. I see my grandson and my daughter and Michael very often, about once a week. I have never known Michael to be anything but loving towards Jed. My daughter is very happy. Jed is very happy."

"Would you say that your grandson is happy with the way things are now."

"Why shouldn't he be, he's with his mother?"

I listened in stunned silence as my father lied again and again. I knew my father couldn't stand Mike because he had no way to understand him. To my father, Mike's near silence every time we'd visit my father's house was enigmatic; it pushed all my father's buttons. My father was insulted by what he took to be a show of arrogance—Mike's speechless staring into space.

"That arrogant son of a bitch," he yelled at me once, clench fisted in his fury. It was long after Mike and I had separated. "Couldn't hold a finger to my wife. He had the nerve to come in here all high and mighty and insult us and stare at us and never say a word. No, he was too good for us. Never said a word."

There was no way to get across to my father that Mike's supposed arrogance was really a wafer-thin defense; it was almost the only protection that Mike had at the time from letting people in too close. Finally, I just stopped bringing Mike with me when I visited Dad. Soon after that, I began to visit less and less.

"Can you see any reason why your grandson would not be happy living with this man?"

"No, none at all."

It took me years to understand what I had seen and heard in that courtroom. Years to know that I had seen my father love me more than he could ever tell me; years to admit that I had seen another father, John, love his son enough to risk hurting me, and years more still to acknowledge that I had seen the fullness of Mike's love, too; that I had watched and heard Mike, every bit a father even then, without either biology or the law to support him in that role, love enough to take the chance and tell the world that he loved someone, that he did love me and this child, Jed, my son.

Of course, you already know the outcome of the trial. Jed was judged normal and healthy and I was judged competent. The court saw no reason to change custody. I was fit enough.

And, after all that, Mike and I married. We had another son, Ari. We tried hard to figure out how to live together in love and peace. And through even more intense fights, through separations, feigned and real, through infidelities and illnesses and moments of pure joy, through all the hills and valleys of a real, human love, we continued for another eight years until we moved to California, land of sunshine and equanimity, and divorced in the winter of 1982. A year later, at the age of fifteen, Jed decided to move back to New York to live with his father, John.

Two summers ago, the whole cast of characters assembled again before another judge to witness Jed's marriage to Danielle. There we all stood— my stepmother, my sons, my lover, my two ex-husbands, their wives, the universe of uncles and aunts and cousins and old friends from the four corners of our lives—all the broken bits and reconnected parts of this crazy-quilted family arranged all together, looking as normal as anyone's. And, without enmity and with the strength of rediscovered love, we wished with all our hearts for Jed and Danielle to have and to hold together all that the future would bring. My son Ari, the best man, nervous yet daring, rose to lead us all in a toast to the couple. "I toast my brother, Jed, and my sister-in-law, Danielle, for what they have taught me about love." And we all swore together, wounds and all, that, as witnesses, we would help them keep love right in the middle of their world.

Parts of Speech

Strong, comforting, manipulative, lonely, caring, loser, loner, clever, funny, enraged, dedicated, depressed, addicted, victim. All the assorted words and syndromes and allusions, all the words that can hold another life in the fragile balance of their syllables. I couldn't stop thinking about words.

When word first broke that Andrés had been arrested in Santa Cruz, we were all relieved. I mean, we who knew and loved Andrea were relieved. Finally, her murderer was in custody, we thought. "The bastard's gonna hang," someone even said. But what we read in the paper in mid-November, a week after Andrea's murder, was English-Howard denying his guilt. "I had nothing to do with her death." I knew that he had confessed to Andrea's mother on the phone. "He called me collect Tuesday night to tell me he thought that he had killed her," Lesley Lane told reporters.

But a few days after his arrest, here he was denying that he had anything to do with it. He even denied the confession. "I said something happened to Andrea and I don't know what's going on. I never admitted to doing it." He entered a plea of not guilty. An editorial on November 22 in the *Daily Aztec* drew connections to the O. J. case: "Many people have condemned him as the murderer even though he hasn't been convicted of the murders. Closer to home, we have a similar situation with the recent murder of SDSU student Andrea O'Donnell. . . . It is up to the jury to decide whether Simpson and Englishhoward [*sic*] are guilty or not guilty. Unless they are convicted of the crimes, no one has the right to call them murderers."

The necessity of doubt. The editorial caught me off guard in the house of certainty I was inhabiting. It surprised me with how sure I already was that Andrés had done it, so absolutely certain without any inquiry, any trial. Lesley said so. Some of Andrea's friends who knew Andrés pretty well were sure. He snapped when she decided to walk, one said. The police had evidence. And the prosecutor, Peter Gallagher, was damned clear that he could prove murder one.

But the house of certainty had deeper foundations than the law and matters of evidence and theoretical predictors of violent behavior. When I crawled under the basement of that house, I discovered something in that dank, stifling space so powerful that it took my breath away. There I found my certainty that Andrés was guilty in the mirror image of my certainty that O. J. was getting away with murder. There I heard someone say, well, just look at them, look at those sneaky eyes trying to cover up an unspeakable act of horror with a whimpering denial and a "feel sorry for me, I only ran because I was black and high and scared." What do you expect? Of course he's lying; of course he did it. And I saw my certainty blanch even more at my own inability fully to resist the inarticulate, twisted idea that one black man convicted was as good as another.

Now we all know that race is a fiction invented in the eighteenth century, contrived by the institutions of medicine and law and religion to perpetuate long after the prohibition of slavery had eroded its more purely economic foundations. And we all know that science has proven that the differences between blacks and whites are less significant than the differences between individuals regardless of supposed race. But, explain this: How come we can still look at the world and see not only difference but pathology? How come we have such a wordless impulse to hear deceit instead of fear? How come the jury selection experts know all this and use it to help shape panels of our peers to include or exclude, depending on whose side they're on, black women who will not be so easily moved by stories of abuse and white, working-class men and women who will most likely fail to accept drug-filled tales of woe?

And how come we see and say and do all this and still think that justice is blind? She would have to be not only blind, but deaf, mute, and without a care in the world for me to ever again believe that a jury trial settles the facts of the case for any of us any longer than the minute it takes to read the judgment itself. No, the only thing a trial settles is that we are doomed; we will forever wound ourselves with the repeated memory that its adversarial aim for the truth can never yield sufficient proof that the target it hits is the only truth to be found.

In the face of my own easy complicity, that editorial and the doubts raised by pictures of Andrés made me realize that he would always be only another human being, not some incarnation of evil that I had imagined a murderer must be, and that I was only another human being, not some prejudice-free saint above the deadening temptations of racist logic that I had imagined I must be.

I think that was when I knew I had to watch.

When I saw Andrés for the first time, he was sitting in court, waiting to be judged by a jury of his peers picked without the counsel of O. J.'s teams of jury experts. A jury picked with the defense knowing that the arguments would be about not whether he did it but only how and why. The matter put to the jury in the English-Howard case was simple enough: Determine the state of Andrés's mind at the time of the crime. Was he high on rock cocaine, or did he knowingly and callously strangle his girl-friend to death? Would the jury ignore what he did and focus on what he thought? How would they determine his responsibility?

By the time the trial began in July 1995, Andrés English-Howard had admitted that he had killed Andrea O'Donnell, but he had entered a plea of not guilty to first-degree murder charges. Why did he kill her? What happened? That would become the focus of the trial.

It wasn't murder; it was an accidental, unplanned, moment-of-passion slaying by a drug user too whacked out by rock cocaine to know what he was doing enough to stop, English-Howard's attorney, Marc Carlos, said. That's crap, the prosecutor countered. "There is no evidence that he was under the influence of rock cocaine or anything else when he choked the life out of Andrea O'Donnell." He killed her because she had decided to leave, Peter Gallagher said. He killed her at the moment when most women in abusive situations are the most vulnerable: when they choose to exit.

Into the fray came the witnesses, the friends, the investigating detectives, the experts with their medical and psychiatric testimonials. They spun stories of a young, multifaceted woman, as admired for her energy and dedication to women's issues as for her fun-loving spirit. They told about a strong, competent, yet caring individual who always helped others. They wove tales of a young man who was a loner on a downward spiral of despair and self-loathing. He seemed a cowardly, scared, suicidal, desperate man, vulnerable to uncontrollable rages that he already had directed at himself. They could just as easily be directed at another, even a loved one, if the threadbare safety net protecting him from the demons within finally ripped completely apart.

Determine the state of mind of the accused, said the court. Figure out what he had intended to do, said the judge. A simple matter, but one immensely more complicated than whether he killed his girlfriend or not.

As I watched the trial unfold I began to think about the arbitrariness of it all. What if Andrés had stuck to his original story, that he had nothing to do with the death of his girlfriend? What if he had had a different set of attorneys, a jury like the one picked for Simpson? Would they have helped him secure his fictions, allowed him to try for acquittal? What made him confess, agree to admit that he had killed Andrea? Why didn't he deny it? There had been no witnesses to this crime. Why didn't he continue to lie?

I thought about the simple tales that could be woven together by circumstantial evidence or bungled investigations into powerful, wrongful accusations that built their own truthful effects on the scaffolding of easy assumptions and incomplete inquiries. Even fingerprints around Andrea's and Andrés's place, even the strewn hand tools found around the bedroom floor, even the splintered bedroom doorjamb and the lack of forcible entry that seemed to point so damning a finger toward the accused lover could be explained away, if you had the right attorney, by the disheveled arrangements of their young, ordinary lives.

Probably the most damning evidence introduced by the prosecution was Andrés having stolen from Andrea's bank account on his run north. That theft made him look calculating, capable of uncaring, even gruesome, deeds. But if he was out of work and running scared, as he'd said, and there was his white girlfriend strangled in their bed . . . Well, couldn't he have stuck to his story even there? Now *there* was a race card waiting to be played.

Of course, there was no race card for Andrés, because Andrés wasn't clean enough. He had that cheap, dirty drug habit of crack cocaine. No Gucci shoes or Armani suits. He didn't deserve a clean excuse. He had had lots of white girlfriends, but no status to justify his ability to sustain that "transgression" except what he himself described weirdly, in the interview with his psychiatrist, as a conscious effort to avoid black women because they reminded him of his mother.

So here we were, watching similar tales unfold on parallel screens, with O. J. saying nothing happened and with Andrés saying what you think you see is not what happened. Finally, Andrés said, "I did it but I didn't mean to." But O. J. persisted. "I didn't do it even if I wanted to."

What I saw beyond the strength of any of the prosecution's evidence, which might have been mitigated had Andrés been O. J., was something that precluded any legal strategy other than the one that defense attorney Carlos pursued. Andrés admitted killing his girlfriend not only because the prosecution was strong and had refused to bargain down the charges but because he seemed to feel some glimmer of remorse.

At least he said he did. I know not everyone can see this, not everyone can accept this. But I believe that Andrés started to think about what he had done. And once he started to think, he confessed. And once he confessed, the only way to get the jury to go beyond judging the sheer fact of his killing to consider the awful circumstances surrounding it was to ask them to enter the labyrinth of intent.

Andrés English-Howard's only hope was that the jury might be willing to accept his drug use as reason enough not to convict him of murder. His attorney had to argue that the evidence was insufficient to prove intent. English-Howard could not have known what he was doing at the time, Carlos said. His mind was too bent by the drugs to expect him to choose to stop strangling his girlfriend. He had been in a state of rage. He was sorry.

It was a dangerous ploy that could and did backfire. Who on the jury could feel sorry for a black man, a drug user, who cut off the life of his white girlfriend just because she nagged him about stealing her change? This is where the war for the truth comes to rest in a trial: What character makes a compelling case? Images of who we want to be seen to be contest with the images of who we are shown to be. Simpson remained throughout his trial a hero who happened to be black; English-Howard remained throughout his trial a black man who could never be a hero.

Into this context the students came with their testimony about what had happened in the days before Andrea's death. Their stories kept in motion intertwined narratives about race and gender to which both prosecution and defense would obliquely appeal. The prosecution portrayed Andrea as a campus leader, a strong, caring woman capable of defending herself against just about anyone except someone who might have the cunning to take advantage of her care. In contrast, both the defense and the prosecution agreed that her killer, Andrés, was "an addict and a loser." But more a manipulator, the prosecution said, than a real junky. The students testified that Andrea herself believed that San Diego was unaccepting of their interracial relationship; the prosecution used that idea to strengthen its contention that Andrés was manipulative, that he had constructed a narrative of racial persecution and helplessness complete with a feigned suicide attempt to keep Andrea from leaving. That's how manipulative he is, said Peter Gallagher.

Whether or not Andrés was a genuine suicidal junky, the defense would have to turn the characterization of him as a forlorn abuser of drugs into a black man sympathetic enough to convince the jury that he may have killed, but he did not murder.

That was the first time I noticed how quickly verbs turned into nouns. Nouns have a peculiar fixity to them that verbs defy. Nouns are things people are or become. Verbs are actions people do. It's the job of the prosecution in a murder trial to make the verbs disappear so that the one who does the killing stops being someone who killed and becomes instead a murderer. That simple shift of parts of speech erects huge roadblocks in the mind's pathways toward reasonable doubt; it stops judgment dead in its tracks. I had to work hard, to listen closer, to hear my own doubts.

I began to see more clearly than ever before that who pays attention to what and why determines the outcome of a trial. I remembered how pleased Peter was with the jury selection. And I thought back, once again, to that courtroom I had been in myself and to the need to tell a story, any story, as if your life depended on it.

Andrés wanted to tell his story. He described how he was so high he couldn't really remember what happened. He was on a buzz, in a daze.

"I was sweating, my eyes were bugged out, the adrenaline was pumping, my ears were ringing, and I was higher than I'd ever been before."

She was waiting up when he got home, he said. They quarreled. He took another hit off the pipe.

"She was going blah, blah, blah, and I jumped on her. It happened really quick. One minute I was at the door and the next I was just on her. . . .

She told me I was hurting her and it just didn't register. I had her. I had her in my hands. I was choking her. It just didn't register. I didn't stop."

Believability creates truth.

The prosecution succeeded; Andrés was convicted of first-degree murder. On October 9, 1995, the night before he was likely to be sentenced to life imprisonment, and days after O. J. had been acquitted, Andrés hung himself in his jail cell. His cell mate turned his back. He didn't watch.

3 Women's Movements

~

Beginnings

In November 1967, the Jeannette Rankin Brigade marched on Washington, D.C., to protest the war in Vietnam. They wanted to call attention to women's opposition to the war and named themselves after the first woman elected to Congress, a pacifist from Montana who had voted against U.S. involvement in World War I and World War II and who strongly opposed the war in Vietnam. Thousands of women participated in the march, spurred on by both their experiences in the antiwar movement and the dissatisfaction those experiences had generated. In Washington, a small group of radical women began to discuss forming an autonomous women's movement. The same discussions were taking place simultaneously in other cities and on college campuses throughout the country.

Women were beginning to express disillusionment with "the movement," as it came to be known. They had typed the memos, served the coffee, distributed the leaflets, provided support. Yet even when their organizing efforts among the poor and disenfranchised in America's inner cities proved more effective than the men's, women found themselves relegated to the sidelines. And there were sexual tensions within the movement. And racial tensions magnified by the sexual tensions. White women complained of being treated like second-class citizens or sexual objects, and black women retorted that no such mantle of femininity protected them from being beaten and jailed as frequently as their black male comrades in the civil rights movement.

Largely absent from the centers of leadership and power that determined movement agendas, women started to feel like cheerleaders for the revolution. And however important it may have been to keep flagging spirits high and emboldened, that was not the role that women wanted to play. A new day was supposed to be dawning, the Age of Aquarius, the moment of perfect equality. To make matters worse, many of the basic issues that women raised—about child care, about family responsibilities, about sexuality, about love and power—were derided as insignificant or ignored. A war was on, racism was the enemy, class oppression was the dangerous dynamic that drove exploitation; we'll deal with those "personal issues" later.

Women wondered where the revolution was going if it did not practice its most radical politics not only in the streets but also in the intimate zones of personal life? Wasn't that what the black revolution had shown? Wasn't it in the arena of personal life that habits got formed and then, old and encrusted, unexamined, worked on the psyche for an eternity of generations, preventing change from ever becoming effective?

Fueled by a growing alienation from their roles in the protest movements of the sixties, many women began to separate themselves out. Within a year, hundreds of small women-only organizations had formed in just about every major city in the United States. Each of these groups differed in some critical way from the others, but in each one, women were struggling to redefine the world in their own terms—in terms that at least included them, menstruation and all, in the outlines of the new world that was supposed to be dawning. It was hard to ignore the fact that the tremulous, forever aproned woman of the fifties, however much a myth herself, was quickly being replaced by another woman, no less mythical in proportion. Braless and proud, this new woman claimed not just a single room of her own, but whole buildings and the central stage of the most public places.

There were demonstrations by a brigade of WITCHES on Wall Street to hex the stock exchange, protests against the constricted beauty of the Miss America pageant, demands to free Black Panther women who, jailed and pregnant, lacked adequate medical care. There were economic analyses of the exploitation of women, critiques of sexual slavery, challenges to the channeling of women's libido. And the sky itself seemed to fall when women, thousands and thousands of them, marched down Fifth Avenue and, louder than I had ever heard, called all at once for "Free Abortion on Demand!" "Free Twenty-Four Hour Day Care!" and "Equal Pay *Now!!*"

I entered graduate school in New York in 1970, intent upon studying international politics and writing the definitive work on debates in the General Assembly on arms control and disarmament. Taking the IRT from Brooklyn to Times Square, I emerged from the subway one densely humid day to find myself in the middle of Women's Strike for Equality Day. It was August 26, 1970. Although I had been active in antiwar demonstrations to a limited extent as an undergraduate, the birth of my first child in January 1969 had changed things. I was determined to get into and complete graduate school, yet not sure how all that was going to work for me as a mother with limited funds and time. And then there I stood in the middle of thousands of shouting women. I had taken the subway from Brooklyn to that promised, that feared, land of women's liberation.

Soon, a group of us, students and faculty, were organizing day care centers throughout the city university system. Forming the City University Wide Day Care Coalition, we pressured the chancellor's office to set aside space and funds to ensure that women from all backgrounds with young children would have access to the facilities we needed to complete our education. We saw it as a woman's issue because the overwhelming majority of those for whom day care was a need were women. Those of us at the graduate center lent our energies not only to efforts on our campus, but also to those at other campuses whose students were primarily undergraduate. The pressure worked; the space was allocated. (Sad to say, there has been a retreat from this position in recent years.)

For many women of my generation, it was an electric, exhilarating, confusing time. Even if you weren't part of the central cast of characters, you heard all around you women asking the same questions: How can I be free? Can I still be loving, caring? The answers that we found resonated troublingly. Women had for so long been associated with the routines of daily life, with all the caring labor of the world, and not with the worlds of doers and their deeds. To think of women as capable of choosing freedom seemed to violate some natural law, to bewilder the universe itself. It seemed to us that if women wanted to continue to feel and to care, then we would have to choose not to act. And yet we felt called to action, to the yearnings of our peers for justice and peace, to the needs of our children and our communities for comfort and safety, to the desire for love and desire, to find a home in the world.

So we tried to combine the two, political action and caretaking. But the equation was unbalanced: the world of politics was skewed toward the men. Some of us felt that it had to be that way, for now. Many of us felt overwhelmed by the enormity of it all; overwhelmed and isolated, as often by other women as by the men who never had to think about balancing the personal and the political in the first place. It really was a man's world.

Then, in those early years of women's liberation, it seemed that we could become doers of deeds only if we separated ourselves from the paths that our own mothers had taken and distanced our actions from anything that resembled mothering in any of its ordinary, traditional guises.

Not that we ever stopped mothering. Apart from rhetoric about smashing the family, we were, I think, simply afraid that all our trying to find another way to work this business of care would still not stop us from disappearing into the familiar, warm, yet enveloping totality of care's demands. Afraid that we would fall in and be gone without a trace. Afraid of wanting to fall in. With no real models for any of this, we kept right on caring and loving, relying often on one another for family, making it up as we went along, donkeyless, slouching toward Bethlehem.

Into the middle of this changed and changing world, Andrea Louise was born in July 1967. Adopted at birth by Lesley and Jack O'Donnell, Andrea lived a mobile and variegated life her twenty-seven years. Though brief, her life's span was full, containing under its arc just about every imaginable, sometimes self-contradictory, sometimes incoherent, persona of a modern woman of the nineties. Artist, upscale retail salesperson, jewelry designer, auto mechanic, tutor, women's studies student, dental assistant, animal lover, self-defense expert, personal trainer, feminist, and committed political activist, Andrea was as much at ease behind the Chanel counter of the chic department store where she worked selling cosmetics and better dresses as she was behind the podium on campus at SDSU where she led student advocates of the Women's Resource Center toward the heady world of new political challenges.

Andrea's consciousness had been raised by second-wave feminists, including her own mother. Jack O'Donnell, Andi's father, left when Andi was only eighteen months old. Lesley Lane, Andrea's mother, moved from her hometown in Petaluma, California, to the Northeast. With her young daughter, Lesley landed in Cambridge, Massachusetts, and set up house in an apartment shared with a roommate. She worked in the MIT medical department, later transferring to the Draper Laboratories at MIT as an administrative assistant, and Andi went to university day care. But Lesley's daughter was always the "anchor" in her life. "Your kids have watched you go through all kinds of things, you're always tight with your kids."

"Andi and I grew up together," Lesley tells me one afternoon in July 1996. It's a few days before Andrea would have turned twenty-nine. I've come to talk to Lesley in her home, in her world. I notice how much more present she is now than she was at the memorial a year and a half ago. And how much closer to her raw feelings than she had been in a long time. We have talked a lot over the months since the murder. But my coming to visit her here, where Andrea had lived, walking through the rooms where Andrea had grown up, sitting on the floor with her in Andrea's room, leafing through the photo albums and the collection of memorabilia— there is something palpable between us in all this private closeness to Andrea. It opens up an emotional channel buried for too long. I look at Lesley's face. I look in the mirror. Two mothers. We can't stop crying. It's such a relief.

Lesley starts to talk to me about Andi, her daughter. "I raised her to help people. I raised her in the Kitty Genovese story. I said, we always run out to help people. You know, there were lots of times we brought people into our house, people who needed help. We always had a house full of people."

Andi delighted and thrived in the makeshift extended family that Lesley had crafted out of the assortment of friends, co-workers, and her boyfriend, Bill, with whom she was involved at the time. The apartment was always full of a collage of people Lesley seemed to collect and repair as easily and carefully as the assortment of discarded things that she and Andi rescued from Boston's urban, middle-class streets. "Junking" she called it.

Lesley and Andi would set out "junking" early most evenings, before the garbage trucks made their rounds, and collect the transformable objects divorced from the lives of their original owners. "I would let Andi help me pick through things and she would say, 'Look, there, Mommy, there's something useful, I know someone who can use that.' And we'd take home old toasters, or furniture, lamps, clothes, and spend time repairing and fixing things to give away or to resell. We could easily find three hundred to four hundred dollars' worth of stuff that we could sell at the flea market, stuff that others had thought was useless."

Mining together the endless possibilities of use and kin to be found in a universe of rejected things, they lovingly rebuilt worlds out of lost objects and lost people, transformed them through the simple ecology of human attention. And isn't family and home only ever that, only ever people and place transformed into intimate circles of blood and belonging by the simple ecology of care?

Lessons about how to help others were all around the urban complexity of the Cambridge in which mother and daughter made their home, collecting things, collecting people. "I taught Andi never to walk away from people who need help. I remember one time in 1971; it was September 1971. Andi, my brother, my sister, and I were walking past Haymarket Square and we heard some glass crashing. There was a large crowd of people gathering. A drunk had fallen through a glass window and had cut himself, pretty badly. He was so drunk. Someone in the store came out to stare. I said to my brother Roger, 'Roger, push the people out of the way.' I wanted to fix a tourniquet on the guy's arm. He was bleeding. Andi is right there next to me, saying, 'Mommy, Mommy, please save him.' Finally, a cop comes by. And then the cop looks at me and says, 'Let him bleed to death, he's just a drunk.' Andi was so sad when she heard that; she couldn't understand not helping. She was crying. 'We always help,' she said."

Lesley moves in and out of the present. Her sentences switch tense. She brushes gently against the loss of her daughter, wonders ever so slightly about whether she paid attention enough. I recognize the signs. No defenses are strong enough to ward off forever the thinnest of doubts. No carefully placed muffler over the heart's ear can ever fully block out that incessantly nagging ronda of what ifs. Never good enough. Never enough.

"But I had to teach her about danger, too. I remember once, in Cambridge, when I was coming to pick her up after work. I think she was six. She was so sweet and so innocent. She trusted everybody. Well, we had a place we always met, at the MIT chapel, on the campus, and I would come to find her in that same place every day, since she was attending MIT day camp. I told her to wait there for me. This one day, I came to get her and she wasn't there, which was very unusual because Andi always listened to me. So I went around the chapel, but no Andi. My heart was starting to pound. I went inside to see if she was there. No. Then I saw a mother with her children sitting where Andi should have been sitting. And I asked her if she had seen Andi and she said she had, but Andi had left with an older man a few minutes earlier. So I ran to get the MIT campus patrolman who was stationed at the student center across from the chapel, and I told him that my daughter had just walked away with some older man and I didn't know who he was. And would he please get on the walkie-talkie and alert the campus police. I gave him the description and then I went into the campus bookstore to see if I could find Andi there, because she loved books and knew the place and I thought I might find her there. At the same time, the campus patrol officer called the head of security, Captain Oliveri, whom I knew very well, and told him Andi was missing. Then he went to search the other side of the campus area nearer the river. That's when he saw the man walking with Andi, hand in hand, across the bridge.

"By the time I came out of the student center, Captain Oliveri was there to meet me. 'They've found her, they're in front of Ashdown House,' he said. And I started to run with him toward the river. By the time we got there, the man was already handcuffed, and I asked the patrol officer to let me walk with Andi back to the station so that I could explain to her what had happened. I knew we would have to go to the station and give our testimony. And I knew that Andi was upset because she had seen them handcuff the man.

"When Andi saw the policeman taking the man away, she said, 'What are they doing to my friend?' I said, 'No, honey, he's not your friend, he's a bad man.' But Andi kept crying, 'No, no, he's my friend. He was taking me to get some books while I waited for you.' When we got to the station, they already had run a check on his prior arrests and found a long record on the guy. He was a convicted sex offender and the campus police captain was so upset that no one had told him about this guy just being put on a work-release program on the campus.

"I knew that I had to teach Andi about how to protect herself. And I had an eerie feeling, even then, that she was only loaned to me for awhile."

In and out of the present. In and out of danger. No different, really, when you think about it, from any story any of us could tell. We might re-arrange the parts a bit, move the sections from here to there. Cut something out. Choose a different town, a different scene. But how long would we be able to hide from the truth?

When Andi was ten, she and Lesley moved to Aston, Pennsylvania, after Lesley had married again. Again, the household was full, this time with neighborhood kids, and with the animals that would wander into their lives and those that Andi would collect. Lesley was "mother" to all the kids—"Andi was the Pied Piper's daughter." The house on Cherry Tree Road, where Lesley still lives, was a place where everyone was welcome. "I always taught Andi, if you take in a stray, you keep it. You don't throw them out. If they want to, they can leave." Some of the kids who wandered into the family felt more welcome there than anywhere else. In 1982, Lesley even adopted two of those kids. Helen and, one month later, Laura came to stay. "When I say I'll do something, it's forever," Lesley says. "It's a hundred-percent commitment, for always, not temporary." Laura came to Andi's memorial at SDSU.

All those experiences must have been formative. Entering puberty, girls and boys learn that they are supposed to conform to the culture's expectations of what they should become. For girls, this means limiting any emerging sense of autonomy that they may have to a territory of no wider scope than the acceptable coordinates of the geography of femininity. For boys, the territory is the scope of masculinity, somewhat wider, but no less bounded. However much those coordinates had been altered both by the history of the sixties and by Andrea's own upbringing, they were still palpably there in Aston, Pennsylvania, in the late seventies. Andrea probably internalized cultural expectations of what a girl should be, but she managed at the same time to tap some reservoir of resistance and self-reliance that she had found or created for herself at a young age. She defied the ordinary conventions of young womanhood that were still in place in the small town where she grew up.

It was the early eighties, and the effects of gender equity in the schools were just beginning to be felt. Andrea followed her dream by attending vocational technology courses for automotive training at her high school. "She wanted to be an auto mechanic," Lesley said. "Her hero was racing-car driver Janet Guthrie." The only female in the class, Andi stuck with auto shop for two years. "She always said to me, 'Mom, *one* of the things I'm gonna be is an auto mechanic.' Andi could never see herself being just one thing, she wanted to do lots of things."

Andrea was multifaceted, always thinking about and trying to decide just how she wanted to be gendered. A girlfriend of her earlier years remembers how, at ten and eleven, they spent hours "playing dress-up with some crazy dresses, building forts, and dressing up Bo [the dog]." The local paper in Delaware County, Pennsylvania, the *Daily Times,* once featured a piece about Andrea and Lesley because of the unusually large number of stray animals they brought home. Another paper featured Andrea in an article about her accomplishments as a student of cars and shop.

Graduating from Chichester High School in 1985, Andrea moved to California to help her grandmother recover from open-heart surgery. She then stayed with her aunt Claudia while working odd jobs and began to think about starting college. It was soon after that, in 1986, that Kay Cline, a supervisor at I. Magnin's in the Bay Area, first met her. "She was fresh out of school, had just moved from the East Coast, full of enthusiasm and sure that she could handle the customer service position we had open. It didn't pay much and that wasn't a problem; she needed a job." Andrea, beset by teenage acne problems, "befriended many of the cosmetic specialists in the store who were helping her clear up her skin. When she realized that the ladies there got gratis products from their lines as well as earning commissions, well, that was all she needed to hear. She wanted to be in cosmetics. Without any experience, and on sheer desire alone, we moved her out of the office and on to the Estée Lauder line [where] she was an immediate success."

Andrea was more than industrious; she was driven by that sheer desire to accomplish whatever she had set her mind to do. And her mind was set on so many different things. After she was transferred to the San Francisco Union Square I. Magnin in the summer of 1987, she and her roommate survived the October earthquake and the following day went to the Red Cross station in the Marina to help others. That night, she called Lesley to tell her that she had finally decided she wanted to go on to college. The earthquake had made her feel how fragile life is, she said. She moved to the Santa Cruz area shortly thereafter and enrolled at Cabrillo Community College in 1990, taking general courses and courses in art and metalwork, supporting herself with several part-time jobs, including caring for an Alzheimer's patient and working in the college art gallery. On the side, she managed her own small jewelry business in the San Francisco Bay Area, fabricating and marketing clever designs of crystal and metal filled with allusive imagery of goddesses and animal spirits. One of her art instructors wrote that her work showed an inventiveness, a willingness to experiment, an attention to detail in the marriage of metals.

You can see in the outlines of Andrea's life all of the twists and turns of almost any young woman's coming of age in urban America in the eighties, the experimentation of the next generation trying to figure out the rules of gender. Sometimes Andrea wanted to be the militant feminist, festooned in Doc Martens, dred-locked and tie-dyed, on the way to the revolution. Sometimes she wanted to be the girl next door. Or the glamor queen. Or the accomplished artist, self-supporting, independent, alone but not lonely. Or even a mother. The marriage of metals.

In this light, she doesn't seem much different from any of the young women I remember who populated my women's studies classes in 1980s in San Diego. They wanted what we seemed to be offering them: the world in all its forms. And if we seemed to insist on the authenticity of some of the world's forms over others, they didn't mind. They changed costumes. They were living in Reagan's America. Whether Republican or Democrat, whether they believed in the necessity of the welfare state or railed against it, they believed in themselves; they believed in possiblities and the future and the power of individuals to fit the world to their desires. Hadn't we given them that?

Yet Andrea seemed to have a peculiar penchant for trying to save people from their own self-destructive habits. She always "helped others in crisis," her mom recalled. "Her main objective was to educate young girls, high school and college girls. She wanted them to know they did not have to be part of an abusive relationship. . . . Since she was little, my daughter was always taking in strays. He [Andrés] was one she thought she could help."

Choosing to help Andrés break his downward slide one last time proved fatal. In court, friends testified that Andrea had decided to leave Andrés and San Diego behind. But not one of us claimed to have been aware that the relationship had become unmanageably difficult. No amount of her sleeping away from the apartment, zealously preaching self-defense, having endless energy for political work, or even those hesitant, allusive conversations that things might be bad at home could convince the young women with whom Andrea worked at the Women's Resource Center, or even the athletic coach who supervised her assistance in athletes' weight training, or any of the professors who saw her daily that Andrea was not in control.

Because the sad irony was, Andrea probably was in control. As much as any of us are. Andrea and Andrés had met in late fall 1992 at Cabrillo Community College. Both activists in political causes, he in black politics, she in women's politics, they became connected ideologically as well as emotionally. Andrea continued to display her multifaceted talents. She excelled at school, receiving numerous achievement awards for her grades, her artwork, and her community service. She tutored kids in grade school, high school, and college, organized blood drives on the campus, helped the homeless. Despite all his bravado, Andrés just managed to get through, already showing signs of drifting from his center.

Largely because Andrea had been impressed with the women's studies program and wanted to pursue her studies there, she applied for and was admitted to San Diego State University. Planning to begin SDSU in the fall term of 1993, she moved to San Diego in June. Andrés came with her, much to everyone's surprise. Her family recalled that she had never indicated to anyone that her plans for her life included him, or any man. School seemed to be all she wanted. Some suggested that Andrés had already been involved with drugs, and that Andrea had thought that a change of location, a new community, would cure him of his habit.

Whatever the reason, the effect was the same. Andrea came to San Diego full of hope, while Andrés arrived in the same place loaded down with the baggage of his past. Andrea wrote in her scholarship application that she wanted to major in women's studies and speech communication to "be able to help our society make a change by furthering education of all people. I feel there is a need," she continued, "to bring about a constructive change in the opportunities for women in America. I believe proficient public speaking skills would enable me to better present my views on subjects related to women and current political issues. There have been many women who have inspired me to continue despite the obstacles I have faced; I hope one day to be an inspiration for someone else." Andrés wrote in his diary about his bitterness, his lack of connection with the white military town in which he felt he was merely biding his time. "I'm at the point where I don't give a shit anymore. I'm sick of working for nothing, sitting up here watching white upper middle class America live large doesn't exactly help."

San Diego seemed to be a place where Andrea had far more going for her than Andrés had. After all, she already had lived there for two years, from summer 1985 to summer 1987. It was a rougher town for interracial couples than Santa Cruz had been. Or at least the more conservative nature of the community of San Diego was available to Andrés as a ready-made narrative with which to explain his inability to connect. He fell into a downward spiral of dead-end jobs and listless days. She pursued her studies and her activism.

Yet she wasn't sure, Andrea wrote in her journal in October 1993, whether she liked San Diego any better after four months of living there. She was busy, though. Inventing a life for herself, and a language of her own, she wrote that events were taking place that were making the idea of her staying in San Diego easier. "I am living with Andrés and despite the roller coaster we have been on relationship wise we, as a couple, are doing fairly well right now. I was going to move out and live away from [him] at Christmas but since [he] told me [he] loves me and has been easier to be around I am giving the idea of staying a second thought. I will see what happens over the next couple of months."

She worked at I. Magnin's in San Diego and continued her magical mystery tour of life, on and off the campus. She got a job as assistant strength-training coach for the Aztecs, the SDSU football team, and connected with other local craft people to continue her artwork. But the biggest thrill came for her later in the fall. "Yippee! And this last Wednesday, Tae, who runs the Women's Resource Center, asked if I wanted to take over next semester! And, of course, I said Yes!!! I am so excited. That is just want I wanted and what wonderful experience for my future as a teacher and organizer. Now I need to work on my speaking, writing, and organizational skills and have them up to par by the time I graduate."

And always the hopefulness about her love. "Andrés was pretty cute last night. He actually walked up and kissed me at one point. We had a pretty good time making jokes and laughing all the time. He really is fun and I sure do like being with him."

But time only brought them to an impasse. They slept in separate rooms. They waited to move back north, perhaps to live apart. We can only think we know what happened, only think we know what might have been.

Still, I find it more than chilling reading one day, while I am combing through Andrea's old notes and papers from her last classes in women's studies—searching for clues, longing for answers to the questions of her life—I find it more than chilling when I come across a kind of warning she wrote. It was not so much to herself or for herself as to and for the women she always wanted to inspire. It's in a paper she wrote about a photo exhibit she had attended in September 1994, just weeks before she was killed. The exhibit was Donna Ferrato's photojournalistic essay on domestic violence.

"Donna Ferrato's photography exhibit is an unglorified version of *Queen for a Day*," Andrea wrote. One photograph seemed to stick with Andrea in particular. It was a picture of a woman called Mary, leaning against the door in her kitchen, crying quietly, talking to the police while her husband is sequestered in the other room. "Remember you were here," Mary says. "Next time I will be dead."

Andrea decided to write about the picture. "I know there are many reasons for her staying and I believe one of them to be that she is 'not supposed to' [leave] or she will be a worthless woman. . . . Media images . . . show us violence with sex . . . and that we are worthless without love. . . . I think that many of us learn that this is what love is however severe or mild our internalization of the combination may be. It may only be the silence, the woman not speaking up when she wants to, I do that, it just seems easier even though I know in the long term—it's not. Or the learning could be as extreme as the choking sounds."

No, there was not one bit of evidence that Andrés ever abused Andrea. No, that is not my point. Neither is it that Andrea knew she was endangered and could find no way out. Nor that Andrés really believed he had no responsibility for what he did or was about to do. The simple point is this: to recognize how clenched and dangerous and lost we are in our own ways within the world when the world seems loveless and without power except for what we bring to it alone.

On the way back to New York City from Lesley's house in Pennsylvania, I feel cold in the middle of July, shivering from the empty, lonely well of loss expressed in Lesley's simple homage to her blond-headed, dimple-cheeked, green-eyed wonder child: "My Andi." She'd said it again and again. I am caught up in this refrain, caught up in the strong desire to be near my own children, my sons, who are hardly children any more. I am lost in all this when I realize that the train has been sitting in the station outside Philadelphia for a terribly long time. Becoming impatient, I wander into the next car and there I encounter the conductor.

"Someone's hurt. Heart attack," he says. "Must have been the heat. A young woman. Sort of heavy. Mother started screaming. They're taking her off the train now. Don't think she'll live."

I walk back toward my seat, tired, numb. And as I pass the window between the cars I watch two hospital attendants wheeling a gurney, struggling between them to cover the body with a sheet. And I see a small black woman, the mother, standing disbelieving but patient, holding her daughter's belongings in a bag like a vessel filled with sacred cloths, gently touching the side of the ghostly vehicle that carries her daughter away.

Two Boxes in Another Daughter's Life

I remember exactly when I stopped believing in god. And where. It was 1966 in St. Louis, Missouri. When I read Nietzsche for the first time, two years later, I didn't see what the big deal was. I mean, I already knew that god was dead: I had killed him in 1966 in St. Louis, Missouri, for letting my grandmother die. How could you build a whole philosophy on that?

That was the year I graduated from high school in Brooklyn. The year I lost my virginity (What a silly thing to say! I didn't lose it. I knew exactly where I put it.) The year after Tonkin Gulf. The year I won the national championship in debate. The year that race divisions in the civil rights movement had gotten so pronounced that the Student Non-Violent Coordinating Committee stopped working with the local church solidarity group to which I belonged.

My grandfather had retired that summer, and he and my grandmother started to plan their trip to St. Louis. Jack Brennan had spent all the years after World War II working as a policeman for the New York Central Railroad, a fine Irish job. His brother, Tom, worked there too. The two Brennan boys delighted in playing on people's inability to tell them apart easily, but their wit in telling these stories was their real charm. Almost every Thanksgiving, while my grandmother, Carol, and Tom's wife, Madeline, were cleaning up in the kitchen, the boys would get around to rolling out the story about the first day they went to work together at the yard.

"Murphy had just outfitted Tom, when I walk in," says my grandfather.

"'Hey, what are you doing here again, I just gave you a uniform,' says he."

"'You did not,' says I."

"'Don't try to pull a blarney fast one on me, Brennan,' says he, getting hot under the collar."

"'I'm not,' says I. 'I need a uniform.'"

"'Glory be to heaven, I just gave you a uniform, Brennan. Ya can't have lost it already,' says he, getting redder in the face. And just then Tom pokes his head around the corner, and starts laughing and laughing, and Murphy is in shock until it slowly dawns on him. 'Christ,' says he, 'two joker Micks in one day.' And we all get a good laugh outta making him guess which one is which."

They're weren't twins. Not nearly. But their red-headed blustery good looks and twinkling Irish blue eyes and fairy-story telling could fool many a person into confusing the two. But not me. My Uncle Tom made it clear to me that he was not my Gramps.

It was the summer that I was deposited at my mother's parents' apartment. I spent that June through the whole of August not knowing the reason for my parents' absence. I don't think I ever really minded being away from my parents. I felt safe and important at my grandparents'. So safe, it hardly occurred to me that I would ever have to live up to the promise I had made to myself to run away from home, out of sheer embarrassment at the failed Catholicity of my family life, if my parents ever really finally did split up, which is exactly what they were doing that summer in the heat of Nevada.

My best friend, Moira, lived next door. She introduced me to Ellen and soon we were an inseparable trio. In matching socks and pedal pushers we filled our days with elaborate adventures in Prospect Park and our nights with ringalievio played all over the two square blocks we claimed as our turf. We caught jars and jars of fireflies and played hopscotch and stickball and dressed up in Moira's sister Eileen's wedding clothes. Well, Eileen wasn't actually her sister. Moira had been adopted, which only endeared her to me more because, as an only child, I gravitated naturally to anyone who could understand how that kind of loneliness felt and who needed to believe, as I did, that the elaboration of friendship could fill in for the absence of biology.

Biology notwithstanding, we built forts in the vacant lot between our houses out of pieces of old wood, discarded metal, and tattered cardboard. We pretended there was quicksand underneath the highest tree and, climbing its branches, challenged one another to jump off and out far enough past the edge of the sinkhole not to slip into its slimy ooze. Or we'd just hang out down at Jentz's, the local ice cream parlor and hamburger joint, where all the neighborhood girls assembled to compare notes on our slow, self-conscious transition into adolescence. We marked our progress by whether and which boys acted strange around us, or by the sudden dis-

Andrea and Lesley, Bermuda, June 1973.

Andrea and Andrés having dinner in Santa Cruz with her mom, Lesley, and friends

*Andrea as a young woman,
Northern California.*

*Andrés folding clothes in their
California apartment.*

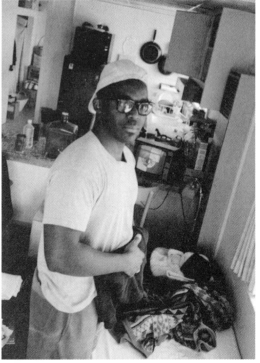

Andrea in metalwork class at Cabrillo Community College.

Andrea and two friends in San Francisco for a ProChoice rally.

Andrea in a glamorous pose.

Andrea at the Women's Resource Center, SDSU, 1994. Photo courtesy of Daily Aztec, *SDSU.*

Andrea with Patricia Ireland and Elizabeth Toledo at San Diego State University, 1994.

Kathy's parents, Edward and Geraldine Jones, on their wedding day.

Kathy's grandfather, John F. Brennan.

Kathy and her parents, Brooklyn, 1955.

Kathy and her debate partner Terry, at the national debate championships, 1966.

Assistant District Attorney Peter Gallagher speaking to the press after the English-Howard murder conviction, San Diego Superior Court, August 1995. Photo courtesy of the Daily Aztec, *SDSU.*

Andrés English-Howard with public defender Marc Carlos at the arraignment hearing, San Diego Superior Court, November 1994. Photo courtesy of Daily Aztec, *SDSU.*

Andrés testifying at his trial. Photo courtesy of San Diego Union-Tribune / *Don Kohlbauer.*

appearance of a close friend in the middle of the night, running, madly it seemed, from the smelly familiarity of giggling girls at a sleep-over pajama party back to the cold comfort of her parents' droning snores.

That was the same summer I was elected librarian of our girls' club. I spent languorous hours cataloguing our treasures with index cards my grandfather had given me and pencils I had pilfered from the telephone company office in Sheepshead Bay where my mother worked. I was establishing the lending rules for what we assumed would be the most complete Nancy Drew mystery collection in all of the vastness that was Brooklyn. Afternoons, I reported my progress to Susan, a younger, siblinged friend, who lived across the alley from the house where my grandparents rented the second-floor apartment. We communicated through handmade walkie-talkies that we had fashioned out of tin cans and string, a device that worked mysteriously but well and kept us in contact whenever Susan's parents insisted that she spend some time at her own house, practicing piano instead of the fine arts of librarianship. I coveted Susan's parents as much as her piano. Any excuse was good enough for me to visit her in the imperial palace, where parents didn't fight incessantly and kids learned to play the primitive chords of "Chopsticks" or the theme from the *Million Dollar Movie*.

Uncle Tom was a regular at my grandparents' place that summer, visiting with notes and deliveries from work for my grandfather to attend to on the next shift. One particular summer day he had seemed to me unusually curious about my comings and goings. I had always liked Tom, he made me laugh, especially when he got my grandfather to unfold tales of their youth together about ditching school to go to the movies or playing some other of their wild pranks on the mill workers at the Pawtucket, Rhode Island, plant where their father worked as a weaver. But the weird way he looked at me that day made my skin crawl. I think I felt his hand rubbing funny on my knees but my mind kept pushing it away. He was going to take me for a ride out to visit my cousins on the Island, wouldn't that be fun. I didn't really want to go. But when my grandmother entered the room and he suggested that I accompany him on a special trip, I found no words to explain to her why not. I giggled my agreement to the plan and thereby signaled my eleven-year-old-girl consent to be his, at least for the next day.

I was OK when we stopped to get some lighting fixtures for his sister-in-law's house on the Island. And even OK when we stopped at his apartment to pick up some things to take to my cousins. But when he took me into the bedroom and sat me down on the bed and started to play with my skirt and asked me to take it off and wouldn't I please kiss him, didn't I like him, well, of course, he wouldn't hurt me, even if he pressed his whole body on top of me, from his bony knees to his bony mouth, what was the matter, why was I so scared of him, don't cry, OK, OK, we would go, then, here, here, watch TV for a while, OK, OK, we'll go, then, and don't tell anyone, OK?

I wasn't OK. While we were driving out to the Island, I gripped tightly to the handle of the car door, scrunched up as small and as far away from him as I could get. I thought about the Catholic martyrs I had read about in the *Lives of the Saints* and that maybe I should jump out of the car at the next red light, but I didn't. I stayed. And then, when we were on the Long Island Expressway I thought, I should jump out now. But I didn't. I just fell asleep. I slept and slept. And I never told.

My grandfather was a hard worker, a recovered drinker, who had sworn off the bottle the year that I had my "miracle cure." "Somehow," as he would tell it, "the angels touched my little Katy. I never thought she was going to live, not with that awful polio. We were all so scared she would die. The doctors said it was hopeless. Paralysis of the throat. Never be cured. But I went to the church and wept and prayed to the Blessed Virgin. I said, Mother Mary, please don't take my Katy. Please, let her live. If you do, I swear, I'll do anything, I will never drink again. And then, all of a sudden, it was a miracle. Holy Mother of God. None of them doctors could ever explain it. Just like it had come, that blasted polio went. But I knew my prayers were answered. And I never touched the stuff again, not even minced-meat pie at Thanksgiving. No, thank you. Thanking God, I am, for my little Katy."

His two heart attacks had slowed him down considerably, but now he was counting the days until his retirement. He and my grandmother were eagerly planning their visit to Missouri, to see old friends who had moved there from Brooklyn years ago for reasons that I could never understand. Who could leave Brooklyn for Missouri? Even though my grandmother was feeling tired—"It wasn't really anything, dear, not to worry, just a headache"—they were determined to go and officially begin his retirement, in style. They didn't even decide how long they would stay or when they would return.

They planned to travel to St. Louis by train, of course. The years of my grandfather's employment had earned him free travel on the rails, and rather royal treatment from all of the conductors with whom he had shared booty from freight cars—the Brennan brothers never minded if a little was sneaked off the back while the engines were in the round-house. Nothing much, just some office supplies, a radio here and there, some paper, cufflinks, shirts, that kind of thing, stuff that filled my grand-parents' apartment with an odd hodgepodge of effects but that gave me endless hours of entertainment sorting, arranging, trading.

By the time they had moved to the apartment off Nostrand Avenue, my grandparents slept in separate rooms. Gramps had to get up at 4:00 A.M. to get to work on time. And he snored, which annoyed my grandmother no end. Actually, he had this funny snore, not really loud; it was like the slight putter of a starting engine. I used to think he was the incarnation of the Little Engine That Could. Whenever I see the cover of that children's book, its smiling puffy face still reminds me of my grandfather. He may have done a lot of things to tease my grandmother—like saving the used matches from his cigarettes in a giant tin can until it was filled to the top, then throwing them away. "Why do you do that, Jack?" "Why not?" But he conceded on the sleeping arrangements. I never really knew whether that was the only reason they had separate rooms, but it still never seemed unusual to me. My parents had separate beds; my grandparents had sepa-rate rooms.

When I was very little, we all had lived together in one big house in Mill Basin, on the edges of what were once farms, in Brooklyn. There, folks had front stoops they gathered on to talk away the humid summer evenings, and backyards where they planted flower bulbs and vegetables, leaving room enough still for clubhouses to be built by us kids out of card-board boxes discarded from new refrigerators or the first TVs. Our house seemed enormous to me. But my grandparents living there with my par-ents and me and the V.'s and their kids living next door and all of us spend-ing the summers in the Catskills together made up for my feeling otherwise oddly alone in a world of good Catholic families with lots of kids.

We played marbles and jacks in the alleyway between our houses, Jimmy V. and I, and dreamed we would grow up to be married one day, probably even to each other. He wanted to be a fireman, but that was out of my league. I wanted to be a doctor, to heal my grandmother's weak heart. She had been all of forty-seven when she had her first heart attack. Or, even better, maybe I'd be a geneticist—I had learned that word in the *Readers' Digest* "Test Your Vocabulary Power Quiz of the Month"—and then I would rid humanity of heart disease forever. That winter I got a nurse's kit for Christmas.

But we swore we would never beat our kids with a belt, the way Jimmy's father did, or disappear into a bottle, like my mother seemed to do. We made a secret pact to run away if things got any worse than they already were. Instead, we just lost touch and drifted into our own futures, alone.

My grandparents' separate rooms gave me better access to my grandmother, who I was convinced really was my mother after all. She picked me up after school. She cooked me dinner. She read me books late at night. I forgave her liking to hang out with my mother at the shuffleboard bars in the neighborhood, when my grandfather was working the night shift, or playing poker with my mother and her barfly boyfriends until all hours of the night after my mother and I had moved to the apartment on Fenimore Street. As long as she was willing to let me have all my girlfriends spend the night any weekend that I wanted, I even forgave her the time she kissed some strange man good-night while I—she must have thought—was safely sleeping in the back seat of the car on the way home from Coney Island one late summer evening. It could have been my mother doing that, not my grandmother at all.

But her dying was a different story. There was nothing about it to forgive; it was just something awful that left little in its wake for me to believe in, and no other ready-to-wear female around to comfort me in that pain, except my mother.

I went to Missouri with my mother and her then husband, Jim, after we got the call about my grandmother's stroke. On the plane on the way out, my grandmother's ghost visited to warn me about what was about to happen. "Watch out for your mother," she said. "And Jim won't be much help. You'll have to take care of Gramps yourself. Bury me in a blue dress." I turned to my mother, who was busy playing solitaire and nursing a stiff whiskey. There was nothing to say.

At the airport we called my grandfather, who seemed strangely calm when he answered the phone in my grandmother's hospital room. "Just get here as fast as you can." I almost thought I had been dreaming the whole thing. But at the hospital, his limp frame at the end of the hall shook uncontrollably at the sight of me. "Oh, Katy," he said, "she's gone, she's gone. She was already gone when I talked to you on the phone, but I didn't want to tell you, didn't want to scare you." And I held him while he cried with sound so raw it scared me with what it taught me about adult love.

I was left in the room alone with my grandmother, still warm. I touched her, felt her face, held my breath to see whether she or I was still breathing. I could swear I saw her chest move up and down. I had to look real close. I leaned down and stuck my fingers under her nose. I thought for sure then that she would open her eyes and start laughing. But she just stayed dead. And she stayed dead all the way home on the train. The whole train seemed filled with only my grandfather and me alone all the way back to New York, him telling me stories about their life together that I had only known about as the grandchild. Only now, I was no longer the grandchild. Instead, I was some reporter he'd met on the train, collecting material for an obituary about some woman I hardly knew. I didn't keep the tapes.

My grandfather returned to his quieter, smaller apartment to sleep in the bed he had become used to. He left my grandmother's room a sacred, untouched place and built a shrine to her of her pictures arranged alongside a statue of Saint Jude, patron saint of lost causes, and a vase of red plastic roses on top of the TV where he watched Perry Como and Ed Sullivan every Sunday night. Sometimes when I would visit him he would cry uncontrollably, which is why, I suppose, my mother stopped going to see him at all. "I can't take it," she said. "He's so sad." She even stopped calling him after a while. But I couldn't leave him alone, not after what he had told me, what he had shown me about the kind of love without which it was possible to die. It's not that I thought I would find that kind of love. Or even that I wanted to. I just respected that he had found it. And that he had trusted me enough to tell me about it. I felt the burden of his dying of a broken heart in a way that, although it made me feel guilty not to spend even more time with him than I did, also gave me enough knowledge not to want to kill myself over the guilt.

But my mother was different. She must have been experiencing two emotions that are hard to keep in the same heart at the same time for very long without going completely mad: intense elation and intense guilt. I know now she was relieved to be without her parents, yet she couldn't stand herself for how that made her feel. I know now she couldn't bear to be without her parents, yet she couldn't stand herself for how that made her feel. So she chose the path of least resistance: she set out slowly and methodically to drink herself to death.

I am sure that language makes both too much and too little out of my mother's willfulness. She actually had a fairly complex, almost whimsical, method to her madness. My grandfather lived for two years after his wife died. He lived to see me marry but died less than a month before my son Jed was born. Soon after that strange Christmas, the Christmas my grandfather's holiday card arrived after he had already died, my mother announced that she and her husband, Jim, were moving into the apartment building where I was then living with my husband and son. I didn't have the vocabulary at the time, but I know I wondered what the limits of care could be.

As I said, my mother had been an embarrassment to me often enough in my life for me to be scared of her being so close. She was an infectious depressive. Still, I hadn't prepared myself for that uncanny combination of listlessness and forlorn drivenness to drink that she allowed to overtake her. That's what I thought, then: she allowed it to happen. Then, my fear of what she was doing made me want to hide whenever I saw her coming down the street.

When I think about it now, I cannot believe the obviousness of her neediness and how frozen I was in a space between that neediness and my own. I don't know any more whether my marriage was already as rocky as I imagined it to be then. I only know that the sight of my mother unraveling before my eyes made me turn for support to my husband. And he, struggling with the demons in his own head, which my mother's drunkenness must have helped reincarnate, had to think fast about what to do; the only thing he could think fast enough to do was to try to help me live by convincing me to keep her away.

At least that's the explanation I have come to now. Then, I felt like I was being torn in half—pulled by Mother into an abyss of childhood returned and pulled by husband into ceremonious loyalty to a marriage we were already losing. By some luck of the draw, I realized that my son was too innocent to be dealt my anger. So I began to let my mother go.

It wasn't really so difficult. Not then. I only wanted her to go away, to no longer wound me. I couldn't see what she had given me: the possibility to live by letting her go and, wounds and all, find my way in the world. It wasn't so difficult to blame my husband for making me choose. I only wanted him to save me. I couldn't see then what he had given me: the possibility to live, with him or without him, and wounds and all, find my way in the world.

I have two things connected to my mother's life that remain in mine now. One is a wooden box of silver-plated cutlery that I remember my mother using only on the holidays. The other is a cardboard box full of photographs of an odd assortment of relatives and friends and random acquaintances, though the relatives have become as random as the acquaintances since my mother died. I wouldn't have even these two things if the landlady, Mrs. Kelly, hadn't kindly read my fear-frozen face on the day we inspected my mother's apartment together, weeks after she had died.

"They're going to be evicted," she said, in the generous way she had of pretending my mother was still alive. By then, Jim had disappeared.

"I thought you might want to look at the place, see if there's anything there that you want."

I wasn't sure about the wisdom of this, but I agreed anyway. And there I stood with Mrs. Kelly, overpowered as much by the smells of my mother's apartment as I was by the shouted facts of her life and death strewn around like so many pieces of plane wreckage awaiting inspection, holding the clues that might allow us finally to determine the cause of the crash. The air was stifling. But the shock of seeing those scattered lifeless things, and the loudness of the stacked plates and tossed shoes and the small still-packed suitcase that Jim had brought home from the hospital after her death made me certain that she was still there. I remember thinking, "Where's the body?" I may even have said it out loud. And standing there, I think I realized for the first time that my mother was dead.

I hadn't seen my mother alive since the day, weeks before, when I had finally convinced Jim to drive her to the doctor's. That last day she had called me on the phone, as she usually did.

"Hello."

"Hello."

"Hello."

"Hello."

"Oh, there you are. What are you doing?"

"Nothing, Mom, just the dishes. Jed's asleep."

"Oh, too bad. I wanted to see him."

"Well, later, Mom, he's asleep."

"My father called me this morning."

"What?"

"My father called me this morning. He calls me every morning to make sure that I am awake on time for work. He called me this morning, but I didn't get the phone right away. So he called back."

"Oh . . ."

"He said, Wake up, Sunshine. It's time to get up for work."

"Um-hmm . . ."

"My father calls me every morning."

"Mom, Mom are you OK? You don't sound so OK. Are you OK?"

"Yeah, yeah, I am fine. When can I come up to see Jed?"

"Mom, he's sleeping, I told you. I'll call you later."

When I hung up, I called Jim at work.

"Jim, you have to come home right away, something's wrong with Mom. She thinks her father is still alive. She thinks she goes to work. Get home here right away."

Then I went down to my mother's apartment, asking the neighbor to watch Jed for a bit. I rang the bell and banged on the door, but she didn't answer. I ran with fear powering my legs down the three flights of stairs to Mrs. Kelly, who had the key to the apartment. I told her what was happening, or, anyway, that I thought my mother was really sick. Together, we opened the door.

There, on the couch, lay my mother. It had been weeks since Mother's Day, when I had visited her with the specific mission of trying to convince her to live. I had tried then to appeal to what I thought was every grandmother's natural desire—to see her grandchild's next birthday. She had cried then. "I'm trying, I'm trying. But what's the point. I just let my own father die, did nothing, let him die. Why should I try to live?"

In the short time since Mother's Day, she must have just given up. And the deflation of her will allowed her body to take over the task of decay and aged her by decades in a matter of days. Her auburn hair had turned the texture and color of a used Brillo pad. Her freckled flesh sagged on her bloated face. She seemed to have both gained and lost weight. But it was the sickly yellow color that her skin had turned and her sad fading eyes that made me cry and hold her and rock her in my arms.

Jim finally came home, and we took her to the doctor. I remember how furious I was that Jim had allowed this to happen. I remember how scared I was that this was my fault too. We sped out to Long Island, to Dr. Berman's office, while my mother alternately slept and mumbled on my shoulder.

"She's not well," he told me. "Her liver is so swollen that I am amazed she is still alive. I can put her in the hospital, but she probably won't make it out. I'm sorry."

So I let her go. I never visited her in the hospital. She never woke from the coma. I made Jim bring her things home from the hospital after she was dead. I arranged the funeral. Jim went to the bar and, about a month or so later, disappeared from my life. Mrs. Kelly gave me the boxes.

"But was your mother really like that?" my friend Gun says to me one day while she is reading this story.

"Yes, she was," I say, thinking I have made it very clear that this is my mother. This young woman, younger than I am today, who left me so that, without her, I could find the way she had helped me in and through the world. This young and vibrant but frightened and lonely mother is my own.

"But she did love you, didn't she?" Gun asks.

"Yes, she loved me, very much . . . in her own way."

"But how do you know, how did she show it?"

And without even thinking, as if I knew it all along but needed only this question to get me to say out loud and in public for all the world to hear the truth, out loud and in public so that I would no longer hide from her, I say, "Because she gave me all the things I needed to live. Even if she could not always be there to care for me herself, she gave me to my grandmother, to others. There was always someone there to care for me. She never left me alone."

Even though I had carted those boxes back and forth across the country, even though I had carried those wooden anchors she bequeathed to me to keep me from floating away, I never knew what they meant to me until now. Instead, I pushed my mother out of my dreams and away from my love. I made her keep her distance until I could figure out, with exactly what she had given me to accomplish the task, how to try to live without her in the world.

Last night I dreamt again about my mother. She visited me in the autumn darkness, the season of my father's death. The room was utterly quiet, so I knew that she was there. I felt her sit down on the edge of my bed.

"Hush."

"Mother?"

Her two hands made their way under the sheets, sliding slowly up beside my legs. I held out my hands to greet her. She took my hands in hers. We locked fingers. The flesh was warm. It was so really warm. I started to talk to her, but my voice was too garbled with sleep. Struggling hard, I managed to say. "It's OK. I'll be OK." I heard myself talking. I wasn't scared at all. I lay there like that for a long time, a long dreamtime. Rubbing her hand with mine, her other hand gently resting next to mine. She rested her head at my feet. But then something happened. She stopped calming me. She moved her other hand across my belly and started to scratch, to claw at it.

"No, stop. Now that's enough now." I said, in a loud clear voice.

And I thought I heard her say, "That's right, Kathleen, be yourself. You don't need to be me. Tell the rest of the story."

And then she left.

If we live longer than our mothers, and most of us do, we have to learn a lesson none of us really wants to admit we need to learn. We have to learn to live without them. And this lesson is hard to learn because, no matter how good or bad we think our mothers are, or how adequate or limited the world tells us that they are, they are the mothers whom we have attached our lives to.

Attachment is the labor of love; it is the work we all do even when we try, desperately at times, to run away. I am attached to my mother for life. And I want to live inside that fact. I want to live inside the fact that my mother's accidental intuition arranged things so that I would be able to let her go. I don't know if I can explain it, but my mother saved me from herself by giving up. Of course, I resented her for that then. Yet I know now that her resignation is what allowed me to love her at all. If she had not let me let her go, I think she would have destroyed me. The pain that I feel about her leaving is pure and simple. I miss her.

For a long time, it was hard for me to feel her loss. I mean, I knew it was there, but I would not let it in. I was angry. I really hated her for dying. I didn't know then why she had had to leave. I walled myself off from the pain. Just recently, I reread some of Anne Sexton's poems. They helped me understand that kind of aloneness that the inability to grieve carves out. I began to see what I had carried around with me all this time.

In this box of photographs is the image of my mother I like the best. The picture shows her in a sexy, Jane Russell sort of pose, angled perfectly for the lucky shot of the *New York Daily News* photographer who caught her off-guard on a busy city street one day, lifting the hem of her dress coyly to adjust the seams of her stockings. It must be 1947. She can't be more than eighteen. She is laughing. Her curly, shoulder-length red hair is lazily caressing the side of her arm. She wears high-heeled black suede shoes that strap around her shapely ankles. She is not at all shy. She's an imp. You would want to meet her. It would take all your energy to keep up with her, but if you did, you wouldn't regret it.

Because, you see, when she was whole she was full of a furious vitality that made my world sing and dance and shimmer with her smile, with the glint of her blue green eyes, with the sun trying to outshine the auburn rays of her hair, with the kaleidoscope of colors that her magician's spells cast on everyone around her. She would shame Merlin himself with her ability to conjure an entire universe of mothers of every sex and shape to care for me if she couldn't. Even the bartenders in Brooklyn.

My mother knew her limits; she was boundless in everything but mothering me herself. If one bottomless glass of her life competed with something else for her attention, her inventiveness enabled her to find a way to satisfy both. Yes, she populated my world with some strange characters, some folks I would rather not remember. But, even if unwittingly, she gave me both the ability to feel comfortable with others and an insight into why not to tolerate fools. Yes, she stayed up and out until all hours of the night. Like it or not, she taught me self-reliance. And she built up in me a deep reservoir of common sense to know that if you needed something you should ask, but you should be cautious about whom you ask for what. She did these things more fortuitously than intentionally. I think back to how I understood my mother then as a situation in need of a structure. But at least she filled my world with people who cared. Maybe it's fairer to say that she did not so much fill my world herself as that she didn't try too hard to keep out of it those who were able to soften the edges of her rough-hewn mothering.

Because the truth is, my mother was an awful cook, and she knew it. So she took me out or to my grandmother's house for dinner. The truth is she wasn't always the mother that I needed. And she knew that too. So she took me to other relatives for warmth and effortless affection and comfort. The fact is my parents fought a lot, violent fights that scared me with the sheer force of their hostility. And she knew that. So my mother sent me to my great-aunt Florence's house almost every weekend, to spare me the sounds and the fury of a deadly marriage. And she knew that I was lonely, so she let me spend as many months in the summer as I wanted with my cousins, who were the five daughters of my father's oldest sister and who had a big house, big enough not to mind one more.

Those aunts and cousins and godmothers and friends and grandmothers whom my mother allowed to mother me, all those women were her lucky gifts to me in my girlhood. And later, though not much later, when I moved out of girlhood into young adulthood, she showed me that friends need to be like shadow kin.

But, always, the dangerous edginess of Mother's life remained tempting. I wasn't tempted then to become her. No, I was tempted to take care of her because she was so needy. That business of taking care of someone who seems so needy makes you feel like the strong one, the one in control, out of danger, even if danger's all around you. Pretty soon you imagine that you're pretty damned invincible. Go ahead, give me a problem. I can handle it. Now you've got the habit. And, like any addiction, it gives you a false sense of security because you don't quite realize how seduced you have become by the elixir of caring. And one day, in fact, you might pick someone to care for who is much more needy and irresponsible than my mother ever was.

If I got hooked early on the habit of caring, my mother at least taught me that the antidote to being overpowered by caring was knowing how to make and keep friends. Friends were people with whom you could share every curve and dip of life's roller coaster and, if they hung on for the ride, trying to help you not fall off, enjoying the highs and the lows, they were real friends, like family. That meant that when the ride got bumpy for them, you had to do your best to reciprocate not because friendship was an obligation, but because it was a bond.

But my mother crammed enough living for two lives into her own life's short span. And, because she never tried to hide from me the truth about the power and danger of love, when she felt that she could no longer have either passion or fun, she showed me what that would look like too.

A wooden box and a cardboard box, easy to move, easy to carry. I have often thought I should discard these things, her ashes. But I cannot. These are the two parts my mother left me of herself: they are her hands and her feet. Her hands, because they touched these forks, these spoons, these knives, and let go, so I can now feed myself. Her feet, because they are the shadows in the photographs of all the places that she left, places that I moved to along with her and, after her, stayed in. Then left again, then returned to stay.

It has always been hard for me to stay in one place. My mother's feet kept moving, and I guess I kept trying to follow her. Only recently have I been able to say "I live here" and mean it. It took my getting past the age she was at her death to believe that I could stay in a place and not die too. Through tunnels of grief and shards of ripped garments I took up my estate as my mother's daughter, not herself.

These two parts of herself my mother left to me, along with an insurance policy that paid for my first years of graduate school after my divorce. She gave me the means to feed myself and find myself and the chance to build a context into which to put myself.

I fed myself different foods and ran to different places in all those days that led up to these. If mother had been born in a different class, she might have passed on a more direct legacy of words, a recipe to tell me how not to blend the world of domesticity and the world of work into the highball mixture she concocted of her life. She was of the era of Anne Sexton, born the same year, almost to the day. I cannot say which chose the slower death. It was painful to watch; it is painful to remember.

But beyond the pain of it, I have the memory of her laughter, her sense of adventure, her insurgent defiance of custom, and her refusal to let me fear her power. For mothers shouldn't try to give daughters recipes without first explaining what my mother explained to me: There is no recipe because you cannot do it alone.

My mother's death opened a door for me and, beyond it, dreaming that there was such a place, I stepped into a world she hardly knew existed. Or if she did know, she had the grace not to tell me about it too soon. It was a wild world of women trying to be different kinds of daughters. We were almost motherless siblings in those days, caught up in the active reshaping of our lives and our histories. I say "almost" because we were busy giving birth to ourselves and to the new mothers that we were fashioning out of rediscovered Amazonian genealogies. These new mothers would, we thought, also serve as our images for the kind of women we were trying to become. But I think, even then, we were not sure that "becoming women" was what we were trying to do.

Many of us had children of our own, which made things even more complicated. We were attracted both to Mary Wollstonecraft and Simone de Beauvoir, to Adrienne Rich and Shulamith Firestone. These women criticized the narrow lives to which many women had been confined, and they seemed to envy men's scope and freedom. Yet they still sang proudly the many accomplishments of women within their limited domains; they still insisted, like Wollstonecraft, that becoming men was not what they were trying to do.

We believed that women had been trapped by socially enforced desiderata that caught them up in impossible tasks of endless caring, but we also believed that caring rocked the world and kept it sane with the steadiness of its rhythms of connection and concern. Already caught up in the available political and moral ideas about choice, we dreamed we might figure out a way not to have to choose between these images at all but, instead, to make the world big enough to hold them both. We were looking for some way to combine "freedom" with "woman" in the same sentence and have it scan.

But it was hard to find the right formula. And it was hard to give birth to ourselves, hard to be mother, father, daughter, son, sister and brother and friend and lover each to the other, all at once. The recognition of this impossible equation finally led us, some sooner than others, to honor the women and the men, however flawed and craggy, on whose shoulders we inevitably stood and without whom we would never have begun this heady adventure in the first place.

That may be why, even now, so many of us still wonder about the power of care, as we stumble on the rocky, manly path to freedom. We are still wondering what kind of daughters, or sisters, or comrades, or mothers, or friends—or whatever metaphor for relationship or connection you prefer—we are; we are still wondering what is becoming of us.

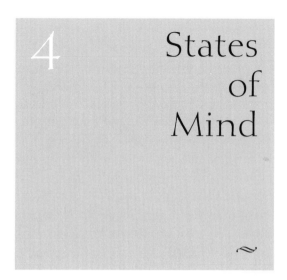

4 States of Mind

~

All Souls' Eve

On Halloween, it seems easier to move between worlds than on almost any other night. It's a time for costumes and carnival, a night when neighbors seem a little less suspicious of who is walking their streets, an evening to remember, to mourn, to honor the dead.

Groups of twenty-five or more kids giggle in the streets near my house, dragging bags filled with candy, sporting the latest masks and gimmicks of the day, speaking in tongues. Within an hour, all the Hershey bars and raisin boxes and Tootsie Pops that I have squirreled away to supply my night visitors amply are almost gone. I have one more handful of goodies for one more set of kids before I have to choose between my options for the night. I either close up shop and hide in the dark or ignore the incessantly ringing front doorbell whose defeated murmur echoes on the wooden floors in my house, announcing the arrival of another wave of soon-to-be-disappointed kids.

But when I answer the door this last time a lovely young girl is standing there to greet me. She is no more than twelve or thirteen and beautiful in her flowing gown of lilac gray satin, sashed at the waist with a braided rope that glances off her hip at a just-so angle. Jet black, her long hair is held in place with a small sparkling comb. The glint of it flickers on her olive taupe skin in the magical evening's light. I catch myself staring at her. Breathtakingly transported; unprepared.

"You look so beautiful," I say, trying to break the spell.

"Thank you," she says, diffident yet self-assured.

I close the door and turn out the lights. Certain that I have seen her before, knowing I will see her again. Especially in the fall.

I like to think I rank among the world's great skeptics about these things, appropriately modernist in my disdain for other-worldly tales, unremarkably grounded. I'm not so sure any more. I don't trust New Age spiritualism. But I don't trust my five senses either as the infallible source of the truths of living. So maybe my skepticism is just fear of gullibility in disguise.

It could be that there really is a place, with more layers, more zones, than the structured three-dimensional one in which we live. It could be that we access it through restricted avenues, detours of the heart, or the shortcuts of madness. It could be that what stops us from doing this more often, what holds us in place, is the simple fact that we are all afraid of having to tell what we have seen when we return from the dead.

Have you ever gone there? In the nightmare moments of a dream, when you feel yourself falling, when you hear yourself screaming, when you awaken as uncertain of your innocence as the reasons why you are still trembling at nothing at all, are you so sure that we are separated from either the angels or the devils by anything more than the thinnest layers of illusion?

One fall night, when I was about fifteen, I remember walking home with a boyfriend down the elm-lined avenues of Crown Heights in Brooklyn toward the big second-floor apartment in a rambling Victorian house on Fenimore Street where I lived with my mother. In the shadows ahead, I thought I saw a man running from the house. Then another man ran after him. A car door slammed and a big, blue 1964 Cadillac sped down the street. I had a sinking suspicion I knew who it was.

When we got to the front porch, the door was wide open. I told my boyfriend to wait while I went upstairs to see what had happened. Climbing the creaky steps slowly to our apartment, I could see that the door to the apartment was ajar. I walked in. It was quiet except for a low moan. I moved slowly into the living room. The ugly green couch, looking drunk, standing on only three legs, sheepishly announced the recent end of a struggle. Scarlet-jeweled pools of blood glistened on the wood floor. The carpet was twisted from people's tangled steps, caught off-balance in the fray. Spilled glasses and ashtrays full of cigarettes littered the room. When I looked down the hall, there was my mother coming out of the back bedroom, one hand holding an ice pack, nursing her swollen eye, while the other adjusted her torn blouse.

"God, Mom, what happened."

"Nothing. I'm OK. It was that bastard Jimmy."

"Jimmy the Rebel?" My mother nodded. A few years earlier she had started dating this obnoxious, soulless man they called "the Rebel." The nickname merely located him geographically in the world, accounting for his thick southern drawl. Apart from that, he was, politically speaking, the antithesis of rebellion, about as miserable and misogynist as they come. He drove a big Cadillac and pretended to hide his crude masculinity, while he thrust himself into my life with loud curses and his twisted, cruel heart.

I could never understand what my mother saw in him. He was an intensely jealous and unbearably mean man and, I thought, just plain stupid. I was only fifteen and I could see right through his efforts to try to win me over with lavish presents and dinners at fancy restaurants. I told my grandmother he was evil.

"Don't worry, your mother's ending it soon," she said.

I'll give it another month, I thought. Then we'll see.

I don't know what I thought I could have done if he refused to leave quietly. I had no simple schemes for how to make him disappear from my life forever, taken away like another empty Scotch bottle tossed into Thursday's trash. But I had never experienced hate before. And I hated him for making me feel the dirty little secret of my loathing him gnaw like a rodent on my heart. That foul-smelling rage rat made me wish all the more that he were dead.

In the meantime, my mother had gotten engaged to another Jim. Although this other, gentler Jim shared my mother's bad habits, he said he adored her and wasn't afraid to tell me and the whole world so. And he never tried to bribe me to get closer to her. So I thought Jim might bring equilibrium to our life. I was even looking forward to the wedding.

And then came the blood-splattered night.

"Why was that idiot here?"

"He came to see if he could talk to me," my mother said, trying to soothe her wounded face. "He said he wanted to wish me well. Jim was here. They got into a fight. Then he ran out. Jim's gone looking for him now."

"To do what?"

"To finish it. No, it's all right. Jim will be right back. Don't worry," she said. More to calm herself down than me, I thought.

"You better go lie down. You look awful," I said.

Then I remembered my date and went downstairs to tell him good-night.

"Is everything OK?" he asked.

"Fine, just fine. But my mother doesn't feel well, so you better go."

He looked relieved at not having to know what really happened and left. Another coward, I thought.

For years after, we continued to see Jimmy the Rebel skulking around the same watering holes that my mother and stepfather now frequented together. Every now and then, a few beers too many into the night, Jimmy would rise up from his seat as if he were about to stake a forgotten claim. But he'd be too stupefied to make any sense and someone would usher him to the door. Then one day, he just disappeared. Soon after, my mother died. Then Jim disappeared too. Just vanished, leaving us all for dead.

Expert Testimony

"So you've got the psychiatric report. Is it from his witness or ours?" Peter Gallager and I are talking about Andrés's psychological profile.

"I have Smith's report," I tell him. "I've never seen the one from your guy."

"Well, I have a whole file of materials. My files are yours, Professor.

"See, Smith switched his testimony at the trial. He changed it midstream. First it was cocaine-induced intoxication delirium. But he got hammered in another case on his 'diagnosis of the month.' Sure, delirium, just for the two or three minutes of the killing. Delirium is supposed to be incapacitating. Not just for a convenient few minutes. So he changed his diagnosis to bipolar coupled with cocaine intoxication. Bingo. I've got him.

"I wanted to get what English-Howard said on the brevitol tape into the trial. The stuff about his hearing her say he was hurting her. And it didn't mean anything to him. But I didn't want to show the video and I didn't want to mention 'truth serum.' So I had to figure out how to get those words of English-Howard's—"I heard her"—into the testimony. And through the pretrial hearing I was able to do that. Smith testified then that English-Howard had heard her. And that he had said that it didn't mean anything. Smith tried to use that as an example that English-Howard's memory was impaired. For just that one little minute? I asked him. That's delirium? He squirmed."

When I return from visiting Peter in the South Bay Domestic Violence Court where he is now working, I have bags filled with documentation from the trial. Police reports, lists of evidence, diaries, correspondence between Andrea and Andrés, a transcript of a videotaped interview with Andrés made at the La Mesa police station when he was taken into custody in San Diego, the autopsy report, excerpts from Andrea's diary, and a transcript of a tape that the prosecution referred to as the "birthday tape"—a rambling, almost incoherent, monologue that Andrés had recorded for Andrea on the occasion of his birthday. Later I add to these a copy of Andrés English-Howard's journal that I found among the court records on file in San Diego Superior Court.

I arrange the borrowed papers around the perimeter of my study like so many pieces of a puzzle I will never be able to complete. Wading through them makes me queasy. I kneel down on the floor for a closer look. The words form a picture of desperation, a contorted pose into which two young people's lives had been drawn. I move around them. And I wonder how I would feel if I didn't know either of these people. I wonder how I'd feel if either one of them was my child. Different angles of view.

All of these documents form an odd behavioral map whose patterns can be construed in any number of ways. They can be read as unwitting clues to the cunning maneuvers of a skilled con artist. They can be taken to indicate the almost mindless meandering of a manic depressive teetering on the edge of cocaine-enhanced chaos without so much as a beacon left in his reckless life to steer him past the shoals. They can even be ignored, dismissed by the jury as a useless distraction on the way to a necessary conviction, the gathered results of public energy and public money squandered on an admitted killer who would have given anything for a loophole. Wouldn't you figure?

I imagine that the combination of poor judgment and the absence of enough escape routes could create, in any life, a tinderbox waiting to be struck. I wonder what keeps us all from going up in flames.

Some time in March 1995, Dr. Clark Smith had been hired by the defendant to assess the state of mind of the accused at the time of the incident. He conducted two interviews with English-Howard in early May while

Andrés was in jail awaiting trial. On May 10, Smith drafted a preliminary report; he sent out a final report at the end June. On the basis of the interviews and all the documentation from discovery that he had reviewed, Smith concluded in his evaluation that at the time of the instant offense English-Howard was suffering from cocaine-induced delirium, accompanied by severe cocaine intoxication, in a longstanding, well-documented pattern of cocaine dependency.

In the pretrial hearing, Smith testified that in addition to his own interviews with English-Howard, Smith had requested that Mark Kalish, a psychiatrist at Mercy Hospital, perform an independent evaluation of English-Howard. On July 7, 1995, Kalish interviewed English-Howard using sodium brevitol. This kind of interview is used to corroborate patient history. Sodium brevitol reduces inhibitions and creates a general state of sedation close to hypnosis. Under its influence one's defenses are down; talk flows more freely. It's not fail-safe; clever folks can still manipulate the situation, even lie. But the drug makes it less likely that a person can avoid making self-incriminating statements.

The brevitol tape was revealing. It would have been damaging for the prosecution to show it. The defendant crying at the recollection of what he had done, who wants that shown in court? Bad enough he'll probably cry when he takes the stand. But that's what cross-examination is for.

On July 31 and August 1, 1995, Dr. Clark Smith took the stand to give his expert testimony in the murder trial of Andrés Lamont English-Howard. He had already set the stage for his analysis in a pretrial hearing that was held on July 18 to determine the admissibility of some of the psychiatric evidence. For some time before Andrea's death, Smith testified, English-Howard had been ingesting cocaine on a fairly regular basis. He was also actively engaged in denial, to himself and others, about how severe his addiction had become. Besides what English-Howard disclosed in the psychiatric interviews, Smith cited corroborating evidence in defense witnesses' statements to investigators, in prosecution witnesses' reports that Andrea O'Donnell had expressed concern over English-Howard's drug use, and in citations from English-Howard's own journal.

There was also evidence, Smith contended, that English-Howard showed signs of bipolar disorder, of being someone who suffered from manic depression. It would have made him more sensitive to criticism, more emotionally fragile, even overwhelmed, by the impact of things under the influence of cocaine. The cocaine addiction would have exacerbated depressive mood swings to which English-Howard already was subject.

At the time that he killed Andrea O'Donnell, Smith concluded during direct examination by the public defender, English-Howard was in a state of disorientation. (Some of the quotations from the trial record are paraphrased for clearer presentation.)

Q. And what about his awareness of time and his . . .

A. His, his perception of time and perception of what was going on in that room at that instant was all centered. Obviously, anyone here would have their perceptions altered by the use of any amount of cocaine, but particularly large amounts of crack cocaine. It's a very, very intense effect of the brain, but also he talks about the misperception of time, that he glanced over at the dog what he thought was just a second, but when he looked back at her, she was no longer alive.

Q. What did he tell you he did next?

A. He said that he was in a frenzy, that he was running around in circles, literally, that he kept looking at her and checking her to see if she was alive, and she did not wake up, that his first thought was to kill himself, and he started smoking more and more of the crack cocaine, but he didn't die, and he also had second thoughts about that. He stated that he was afraid of what his mother would think if she found his body dead from a suicide attempt. He said he's also thought about jumping off the balcony, by the way.

It all added up, in Smith's assessment, to being in such an altered mental state at the time of the killing that Andrés could not have acted with intent to kill. He just got carried away. And then he freaked; he was in a panic. And tried to cover up what he had done. That was what explained the plastic bag and the cord around her neck. Well, yes, that did take some thought, but, no, it was not inconsistent with cocaine intoxication. Done in a panic. A pathetic attempt.

That was the defense case; the prosecution had a different story.

But that's just so much interpretation, isn't it, Doctor? Different theories, different approaches, different conclusions. Not really an exact science, is it? And all based on self-report. I mean all based on the words of the defendant himself, right? OK, so call it patient history. But, he could make you think what he wanted to, if he were smart enough, couldn't he? Oh, I see, your experience would tell you differently. But you didn't even record the session. You just have your notes, your ideas about what was or was not important about what he said in your interview of him.

Sure, I know about his journal. But if his journal was so important, and you had it beforehand, why didn't you incorporate it in your final report? You testified to a lot of things from the journal, but all you did for the final report was fix typographical errors? You just saved it for the trial, huh?

Sure, you had another report from another psychiatrist. But you already knew what you thought before you asked Dr. Kalish to do that interview, didn't you? Ever hear of examiner effect? I know; you try to avoid it. But, suggestibility, eh, Doc? Psychiatry's not an exact science. You could be wrong. English-Howard could be "pulling it," to use his own phrasing. Trying to get out of another jam. The jury won't buy it.

The jury didn't buy it. In less than twenty-four hours after closing arguments, they found the defendant guilty of murder in the first degree.

All those records surround me now, all the reports and testimony and bits of evidence. I read them again and again. Slowly, deliberately, checking for inconsistencies, looking for escape routes.

Would I have argued it differently?

Objection. Speculation.

Sustained.

Would I have interpreted it differently?

Objection. Calls for a conclusion.

Sustained.

That's all beside the point.

As though it were some strangely broken record, I keep hearing Andrea's voice: "You're hurting me." I keep hearing Andrés's voice: "She was my conscience." A dirge unstilled either by judgment or by death.

> "She knew what to say to me to make me think."
>
> "You miss her?"
>
> "If I could, ah, if I could switch places . . ."
>
> "Um hum."
>
> "I would do it."
>
> "All right, um, I'm going to count to, ah three, and when I count to three I want you to close your eyes and take a little nap for me, okay? One . . . two . . . three . . ."

She Was My Conscience . . .

DR: "Are you feeling a little tired now? Notice that bitter taste. Yeah, OK, count for me backwards from 100."

ANDRÉS: "Yeah, OK 100, 99, 98, 97, 96, 95, 94 . . ."

DR: "Say it a little louder . . ."

ANDRÉS: "85, 84, 83, 82, 81, 80, 79, 78, 6, 5, 4 . . . I'm sorry . . . 48, 47, . . . 13, 12 . . . I'm as depressed as hell."

DR: "Why, why are you depressed?"

ANDRÉS: "Just read what it says in my jacket, read my jacket . . . 10, 9, 8, 7 . . . Hell and high water . . . Born in Cleveland, Ohio. One night, out of the blue, get a phone call, a person says, 'Hey, I'm your father.' Next day, on the plane, my brother and I, flying out to . . . California . . . New stepmom, I'm fourteen or something . . .

"Went to high school in Santa Cruz . . . yeah, I had a steady girfriend, Christina. I was her, uh, her first black boyfriend. Her first boyfriend and first black boyfriend she'd ever have . . . She was naïve, gullible . . . Basic low self-esteem situation. Parents loved me. I couldn't come into the house. . . . Basic interracial relationship. After high school, got a job at McDonalds, worked my way up to manager, became a tyrant—stoked on my own power, just stoked on myself, had a cute girlfriend, hung out with the manager, had a motorcycle, a sports car.

"Oh, yeah, I'm definitely a megalomaniac. I did whatever I wanted to do, always control my relationships. It's just, ah, just my personality is pretty dominant . . . I had a way where I would, I had, I have a way of where I find women who are, ah, who need something. Who are insecure, or don't think, they don't think they're pretty, or something like that. I find a fault . . . And then, I cater to the fault and make them feel good, loved, feel good about themselves and then I get bored and sabotage it.

"Andrea and I met at Cabrillo College, a JC up in Santa Cruz. Yeah, in a weight room . . . I thought she was a stud. She was in there working out and teaching other people to work out. I was impressed, saw her working out in the gym. I was working out. I was doing some competitions, some power-lifting competitions . . . And I was impressed with what I saw. Basic physical attraction."

DR: "What was her fault?"

ANDRÉS: "Well, at first, she's, she, first she would seem to be a person who, ah, who had it all together, and knew what she was doing, was motivated and focused. But it turns out that she had, ah, that she had a fear of being, ah, she had a fear of being, ah, being left. She had, ah, she was scared that someone was going to get with her and just, ah, use her and leave her, so she made a point that at this point in her life she was going to, um, get with someone she loved and work it out no matter what happened. She was going to work it out. . . .

"Oh, yeah, my favorite drug of choice was, ah, marijuana. Yeah, I was doing cocaine, casual use—a weekend warrior. It never became a problem, between me and Andrea, until we came to San Diego. Well, basically, San Diego turned out to be a nightmare for both of us. We, she had, she was having a hard time in school—cause it was a lot harder than what she thought it would be. Um, for me, it was being in a city where I had unlimited access to drugs and, and my, my motivation was to, um, to just to get out of Santa Cruz, where it was too easy. Crank school and get on with it, and get on with my, my work, and helping my, quote, my people and, and then being a role model for Mexican kids and black kids.

"The cocaine use got out of control in San Diego . . . I was a closet drug user. I hid it from Andrea. Oh, definitely, definitely. Because, ah, it wasn't the situation where she and I were, were, both, both doing dope . . . She was motivated. She used to enter a thing and I was trying to do my thing and I was having my . . . I had a little white weekend . . . She didn't know about it for a while. I hid it from her really well . . .

"When Andrea found out, she figured she could fix it. She thinks she could work it out. She'd come to a point in her life where she, where she, uh, she, she figured she was sick of going through one boyfriend, one boyfriend to another boyfriend, . . . god, I'm feeling totally starry-eyed . . . She never gave me money to buy crack, well, not initially, not until I lost money . . .

"I was hustling Andrea. I used her ATM card to get money. I was on a rampage. I was just going for it, she would be gone to school all day— school for me had, was, was, was shot. . . . I had already figured out after the first year that it wasn't working out for me. I was too caught up in hating San Diego, and um . . . I would basic, I basically hated San Diego. I didn't want to come to Southern California. I, uh, never really liked Southern California. I was more comfortable in Northern California . . .

"The day Andrea died ... I remember ... I remember waiting, waiting for her to come home ... I remembered waiting for her to come home and there was a ... I'm sorry, I've been so upset. I am sorry, Mark [Kalish] ... Waiting for her to come home.

"So I waited for her to go to sleep. And then I could take her ATM card and go get high. We were at this point, we were, ah, at this time we are, ah, we both knew, we both knew that I was, I was fucking up and, ah, but we are both, both fooling each other into, into believing that I could ever, that I could ever done crack ... I waited for her to go to sleep. And then I grabbed it. I rummaged through her backpack and took the card and, a, and took off ... I was totally ripping her off. Well, I, but I, I, I fucked it up so much that, that it didn't really matter. I, I figured, I figured, I'm so, I'm sorry, Mark.

"I went out to a, I went to a ... I had, had a hub. I had a place I went to ... Went and ah, bought a dub sack. Which is like a 120 or so dollars in it. It's dope ... it's to smoke up. We're, we're, ah, we're, ah, leaving, when we were leaving, we're out of here. ... We were leaving in the ... we were leaving fucking Santa Cruz, San Diego. I like, I don't know, six weeks or so we're out of here and ah ...

"I hung out for a while. ... Smoked some with the guys. ... Got kind of pissed off and deliberately burned this guy's hand with the pipe. ... I got pissed off because I felt there's no way I was, I was a, was a coke head. ... Pissed off at myself. Totally. I was coming ... I feel like, I was, I was, I was fucking up out of my head. ...

"Puffed some herb, puffed some crack ... and, um, hopped a cab and went down, come to the house, and got back to the house, expecting it to be another weekend ... And, um, I knew that I had to come in basically in, and ... then I had to, ah, I had to, um, basically calm her down and, and her just, you know, basically, I, I would tell her what I was doing, what, what I knew she'd want to hear. ...

"Andrea was up. We got into it. She knew what I had done ... Another weekend, you know. I was a weekend warrior. I was looking at life. You know, during the week, being a Joe Civilian. On the weekend, by myself, I was a, a dope fiend. But I ... I never accepted the fact, fact, the fact that I was a doper. It's not like me—I'm too smart. ... I could always stop when I wanted, whenever ...

"Came home. Had, ah, I had more dope than I have ever. I bought, we were leaving and like in four weeks . . . We're out of San Diego, both of us are . . . we're stuck. I was . . . I was . . . wasn't sure if she would, if she and I were going to stay, stay together, I'm sorry . . . totally sorry. I didn't know if she and I were going to be staying together, but I, I knew that I, I knew that I had, had [this] problem at the same time I um, was, was denying. I was rationalizing to the point where, where it was like another person was doing it. . . .

"And I, uh, came in knowing that she'd be pissed and she was, ah, and um, she, she was up and we went back, went back and forth . . . We didn't really argue . . . She knew what, what to just say, what to say to me to make me to re-respond. She knew . . . what was really important to me . . . She was my, it got to the point where, where she was my . . . was my conscience. . . . And Andrea knew what to say to, um, to make me react . . .

"I went in, I went in to her room and, and wanted to shut her, I wanted to shut her up . . . And I went to her to basically tell her, I was going to give her same, just, just, the same drag . . . to basically shoot some bullshit at her . . . Basically, I knew I could, I, I, I could, I could calm her down.

"She was . . . she was, ah, she was going to do anything she could to keep this relation, this relationship together. . .

"I went in there . . . and . . . I sat there then I . . . I stood in the doorway. I looked at her and she was talking to me. And she kept saying the one thing she could say to me that, um, that really made a difference was telling me to take responsibility for, take responsibility for my, my actions. . . .

"I just sat there listening to her and I wanted her to shut up. . . .

"So the next thing I, I knew, I found, I, I, I was on her. Like, like, like, I grabbed her . . . I, I grabbed her neck . . . I wanted her to, I wanted her to shut up . . . She um, she, she said, um, I, I grabbed her neck. . . . I, I just grabbed her. . . . Started to choke her. . . . It shut her up. She was like my, my, my, she had become my conscience. . . .

"And I grabbed her to shut her up. And she told me I was hurting her and I, it, it, did, I hear that. I mean, it didn't, it didn't mean anything. . . .

Imagine it. Time stops. Frozen in the haunted present, the hands of the clock shocked still by the sheer force of your hands holding that warm life in the unfeeling vice of your grip.

Imagine it. Hands around her neck. She's crying. Hurting, you're hurting her. Not noticing, not caring; pushing your buttons. Doesn't matter. Just shut her up, make her shut up. She's your conscience. Make her shut up. No, don't stop, don't, stop. Pushing your buttons. Who does she think she is? Look at her. She just keeps talking. She keeps saying the same thing. She pushes. Take responsibility; take responsibility for your actions.

Doesn't matter. You're too smart. Hurting her. Doesn't matter. Making you take responsibility. Just shut her up. Your conscience. Want her to just shut up. Take responsibility. Shut her up.

Feels like only a second has passed. Happened so quickly.

I was, I was still strong. Just shut her up.

She's not moving now. Not talking. Now.

First person I've ever met that, could push my buttons . . . She knew what to say to me to make me think . . .

Not moving. Not breathing. Oh shit, oh shit. Gotta get outa here. Got to cover up, get something, get a bag, cover her head, grab that cord, wrap it around her neck. Cover her up. Get outta here.

I've just, I've been, I just, I just been, I've just been around . . . And I know these things. I know. And, and . . . she was not breathing at all. I looked at her, she wasn't breathing . . .

And then you call her mother and tell her what you did.

Because, as fucked up as it would be, it'd be better for me to tell her that her daughter was dead than having . . . some stranger . . . do it.

"All right . . . I'm going to count to . . . three, and when I get to three I want you to close your eyes and take a little nap for me, okay? One . . . two . . . three . . . "

She knew what to say to me to make me think. . . . If I could, ah, if I could switch places. . . . I would do it . . .

Trying To Get out of Another Jam

Filled with the ordinary vices and self-consciously precious thoughts that any of us think when we think we are writing to ourselves, English-Howard's journal records the year before Andrea's death, ending about one month before he killed her.

11/23/93

I've put off this first entry as long as I could. I don't need to go into the

events which led me to be here in the military world of San Diego. . . .
*Here's the theme of this book: FORWARD NOT BACKWARD. Let's see
what happens.*

12/2/93

*Here I sit in beautiful Del Mar with less than a $1.00 to my name. Rent's not
paid.* . . . *Andrea and I got into a fight over this shit but also over the fact that
it's Dec, and I'm broke again.* . . . *It's December and I can't pay my rent again,
it's December and I'm hoping and making plans to recover a lost fucked up semester in school.* . . . *I'm at the point where I don't give a shit anymore. I'm sick
of working so hard for nothing. Sitting up here watching white middle class
America live large doesn't exactly help.* . . . *Starting next year and I'm not bull-
shitting at all I'm spending no money at all on anything except* bare *necessi-
ties . . . work pay bills and save all the rest of my money. I'm not going through
this again!!*

12/2 cont

*Will I or won't I? That really is the question. Time and time again I
find myself asking these questions. Looking for that center, looking for that
easy way and yet not being about to work and change, understanding the
unlimited potential that I possess. Oh yes, I am the great pretender. No
one knows that more than me and the question is will I ever be able to
completely give my trust to anyone? Don't know. What I do know is that
I'll never really be happy until I have some serious success in my school -
career.* . . .

12/16

Phoenix,

*I've cut my hair and am taking on a new militant stance or: dealing with San
Diego. I haven't called my family and they haven't called me. I don't have anything to say only bad, all bad. I'm not putting forth one hundred percent effort
and I know it. But on the other hand in the following weeks I've got to get a job,
plain and simple. I really can't miss any more school. Last week slipped and
smoked again, and as always I didn't have fun only got pissed and wished I had-
n't done it. So here I am one year later and I'm in the same boat as last year. I'm
with Andrea but not completely. I don't know if we'll ever have that complete.* . . . *but just her loving me all the way and my not being quite at my next
step.* . . .

Andrea said something to me last night that in spite of myself I had to listen to. She said that I came down here and started out with my bad attitude and bad things are happening and I get surprised. In a way that's true. I really don't like San Diego and I don't keep it a secret. I don't care who knows it. On the other hand with a little networking and some reaching out I could trip over a few opportunities. . . .

12/18

Should I stay or should I go? That is the question. . . . As far as my staying in San Diego or not it depends on how willing I am to putting in major work. I don't think I can give up this easily. . . .

12/22

Well, I'm still here!! . . . Okay here's the scoop. I just got paid from Del Mar and decided to call the Chevron Station to check the job situation. I got the job and celebrated by smoking. I pissed off some cash. Same old same. Anyway, I go to the post office and what do I find in there but $100 from my mother. . . . Needless to say I was once again reminded that people are depending on my success. I've got to take that final step and accept the responsibility to my loved ones. So I'm staying and working 6 a.m. to 2 p.m. Mon-Fri and I might work every other Sunday. . . .

12/28 . . .

Andrea and I are coming closer together in spite of ourselves. It's really amazing but also true that I'm at my best when I['m] really busy and productive. . . .

12/30/93

Well, this year has been crazy and I can't say that I'm sorry to see it go. It would seem that Andrea and I are slowly growing closer together and as we stabilize our financial picture our personal lives will improve. . . . And of course I'll be hustling two jobs all summer. I've got to start writing. The Ad Lit class I'm attempting to add will help expand my reading list as well as giving me some writing time. Here are some topics for future short stories . . .

—dealing with white women

—school, drugs, family, children. Preconceptions within society.

Throughout my writings I'd like to stay within my framework, the theme should cover basically the story of my life.

1/94/7 [*sic*] What?!!?

Here's the scoop. I'm buying a truck from the station for $430. By my

30th birthday . . . All that sounds pretty amazing considering that I truly didn't think I'd be here at this point. And if that weren't amazing enough, Andrea and I are quietly, calmly coming closer together. . . .

3/4/94

Rampage!! *One step forward, ten steps backwards. . . . I'll deal with this and move on to the next level . . . I know what I'm doing to myself and can only hope that I can reverse the trend and put in another 30–40 years . . . I'll make it and see my 70th birthday . . .*

3/22/94 . . .

I do love Andrea, I love her drive, her determination and her conviction. I need to have qualities such as these. . . .

Words written with no certain meaning can now be mined and metered and scanned, like all diaries of the dead, to draw a deathly diagram that measures the arc of an aching soul, to gloss, however fleetingly, in a hidden moment of self-congratulatory arrogance, a sadly suicidal wish for discovery and judgment and redemption. Then it was a confession too ashamed of itself even to tell the truth; now it's a court record, a criminal document, a latent print of the soul.

From late January through August, Andrés's journal records a slow descent into increasingly erratic behavior. More and more drugs, more and more lies. It's easy to paste it together into a somber-toned mosaic of despair. You can see the cracks and fault lines, the self-deception and fear that led him to feel both elated and defeated by his own cunning.

Here's Andrés happy to be starting the semester at school, again full of hope. One week later, he's in the middle of another "rampage," a drug binge, another self-lecture, another promise to quit. And then, again whole, wholesome, visiting his mom, feeling "outstanding." All followed quickly by another broken promise, another binge, until the mania intensifies around May, his birthday.

5/21/94 . . .

This is really crazy if you just stop and think about it for a second. My mind is going to waste and I'm not really trying to stop it. That old analogy of people being fascinated by death and destruction. You can't just drive by a wreck, you've got to stop and look, you have to. That's me and my body, I'm doing what I can to tear it up and though I know better I just watch and wonder at the car-

nage . . . I'm truly confused by my double life. Why do I need it what purpose is it really having. Am I just dropping the same crap that "they" all drop. It sounds like it. What's wrong with making it. What am I afraid of. . . .

Sliding. A week earlier he had been stopped by a cop in Imperial Beach. Doped up, driving a friend's borrowed car, he still talked his way out of an arrest. On June 3, 1994, he was riding with a friend on his motorcycle. The police take him in for possessing a small amount of rock cocaine, but don't charge him with any crime. Stoked. He keeps moving.

August.

I know I'm addicted, but what is it that gets me going in that direction. . . . The dope must stop!! I mean do I have to get thrown in jail or what? I've got to get my drug shit in order. If I don't go to jail I'll probably get killed or die on an O.D.

September.

I've got to deal with Andrea as a person . . . I said that I planned to take our relationship to a new level and I meant that. I'll have to sit her down and explain to her why I do the things I do. In particular will be my always threatening to leave her. Something I know I got from my fucking father. The more I try not to be like him the more I find myself acting just like him. Andrea is trying very hard to make this relationship work and I'm doing all I can to pull it apart. I know I'm capable of doing what needs to be done in order to make this work. I know how to destroy.

October.

It's late and not good. Not good at all . . . Andrea. Yes, you could say I'm putting her through the wringer. Maybe just . . . A LOT!! . . . I'm on the quiet end of crack right now and I made Andrea a promise to deal [with it]; she won't take much more and that's for sure. I'd say she's at the wall about now.

It's all there if you read it in a certain order. Maybe you can even feel his desperation, feel how he feels trapped. In his head. "Just shut her up." Wants to get out; tries, can't make it. "It's catching up with me." Needs help, knows Andrea's giving him all she can. "Can't stop." Needs what she has. "I do love Andrea, I love her drive, her determination and her conviction." Can't give it to himself. Can't get out. "Calm her down." Not out of the relationship, but out of his own self-created trap. "Just leave it all in San Diego."

But, did you forget what he did? No, well maybe you wondered, for just one second ("*It happened so quick*"), whether he deserved what he got. [Emphases added.]

Only that's not the point, is it? The point is, you've entered. Now, how will you get out?

The Birthday

A few days after Andrea's body was discovered, Bethany K., a longtime friend of Andrea's, was helping Andrea's mother collect Andrea's belongings at the apartment she had shared with Andrés. As they were packing things up they came across an audio tape in the player in the room. When they pressed the button, on came a voice they recognized as English-Howard's.

"Okay, it's four in the morning . . . 5/20/94. I'm thirty years old today, we just finished having one of the biggest, the stupidest fights, and we were having them all the time, since I was a little kid anyway. I'm just gonna talk to the person that can . . . Miss O'Donnell . . . see what happens . . . just gonna hang in there. Try to deal as best you can make some sense as to what is going on; um, basically, I spent my entire life trying not to be like my father."

It was the birthday tape. Like some strange, stream-of-consciousness audio diary of his childhood memories, Andrés wandered from one event to another reminiscing about his disjointed youth, searching for some coherence or explanation for what had happened to him, for who he was.

"And time and time again, 'cause I was the oldest kid . . . I'm gonna forgive my stepmom, who for the longest time I feel like I considered my mom . . . you know, [who] was Mom, she was this person I saw a couple of times a month on weekends, and when I fucked up [as] a little kid in Cleveland. So, of course, I never told her I loved her. . . .

"We hardly ever saw her. And it was kind of weird . . . the day after, maybe two days after uh, . . . Mom's house one weekend we get this mysterious phone call. Mother calls to the bedroom. Go in here, talk to your father. I had no clue who this person was. You know, get on the phone, the usual we, uh, you know, fine . . . yes . . . good . . . good . . . good . . . OK, you know; this is your father, you talk to him, you know, I never recognized anything . . . I don't know, though, we wound up on a plane to Cleveland . . . And then, uh, we're coming into L.A. . . . Meet Nancy . . . 'Cause she was supposed to be our mom now. . . ."

In and out of the past he runs, looking for an explanation for his life. "I'm trying to . . . so you'll know, what the hell brought it on . . ." Groping for some reason he can use, some excuse he can give, some way out. He must be tripping on the past, moving maniacally from place to place. Remembering. Getting caught up in the smells of food his mother cooked and the feel of the tiny apartment she shared with her boyfriend in Cleveland. Recognizing the missed embraces. "No real imprint or figure in my mind. Until that night after my Pop called." Then, wandering down the halls of the glitzy two-story California house he lived in with his father and Nancy. "Right behind our house was the L.A. riverbed. That's right, I remember that." And, after that, moving back to Ohio, then to Louisiana and back to Los Angeles. To the time his father shot his stepmother, Nancy.

"And then we moved—then we fucking packed up everything and then drove back from Louisiana to L.A. And we settled into the fucking hood in L.A. . . . This is, you know, late seventies . . . I remember the day he [father] came in, we were there, we were eating, we had television, Mary was there. . . . Was it Mary? It was Mary, and it was . . . the other one. Mary. Was it even Mary? But anyway she was there yelling when I was there. We came into her room talking about her and hear her arguing with him . . . and then we hear that 'pop.' I knew what it was. I had no idea how I knew, I just knew. He walked out . . . and said good-bye to everybody; too much. . . .

"And I went in her room—I think right after . . . before Mary did. Went to Nancy. She was holding her head. She was holding her head, laying on the bed. And Mary freaked out—went to call the police. . . . I remember grabbing the phone, taking the phone from her, calm as hell. Giving the dispatcher all the information, totally calm. . . . I remember going to court, I remember what happened. . . . And I wound up living with my grandmother."

He's trying to find a way into the present. He's talking to Andrea.

"Why am I telling you all this shit. I don't know, uh, I had to think about the past. I miss . . . my present is weird. I've always lived either in the past or in the future. The present is something I deal with—I don't know, it's weird." Through his youth, his years in high school, the good times in Santa Cruz, the close friends, adjusting to the places he finds himself in, adjusting so well he becomes part of the scenery. "I mean, I just went to— I did this full Zelig big time. I'm not sure you ever saw that movie or not. It's a Woody Allen movie. . . . It's a movie where this person was a Zelig, was a person who would become whomever he was with . . . he would physically, you know, everything, become like the people he was with. . . . So when we first got to Santa Cruz . . . being fucking full Zeligs, dude."

Searching for connections. Old friends, girlfriends, drinking, working hard, and partying harder. "Why am I talking about all this shit? I'm talkin' about it 'cause I, 'cause I miss those times. I was in those times, I was stoked . . . I loved my . . . You know, as fucked up as my whole childhood was it was pretty cool but I'm trying to figure out what is my problem with my—I mean I've got my own thing with relationships. . . . My relationships with women—my relationships throughout my entire life were mostly with women. Those have been the only positive relationships I ever had. . . . And I don't know, babe. And I wanna, I wanna be able to open up, I wanna be able to fuckin' cry out, I want to be able to be everything. I just fuckin' can't."

Caught between the need for love and the need to be his own person and afraid of both.

"I never make the same mistake twice. And that's based on the fact that I sat there and watched my father beat my stepmom, Nancy—like 'cause she's been my mom for a long time, for love, and wish I was in touch with her right now. And my family sucks like that, you know. I mean I really wish I had my family with me. I wish my family was a strong together unit that could be rallied around me and be with me.

"And, you know, and, I'm like, you know, I always respect love and, you know, I'm, I've been forced to—I'm the oldest kid and the one who's been, you know, who's, who's supposed to be all these things. And that, and, and, it's just weird, it's like a weird self fuckin' weird pressure thing happenin', you know. It's like not really pressin' me but they are. And no one really, you now—it's like, but then again, they have that whole thing where I'm a black male so I don't, if I don't succeed, no one's gonna—they'd be surprised, you know. You know, even though my, you know, even though I am capable of doin' whatever I want to in, in this world, if I don't do it, you know, well, you know, it's just another black guy who's just not doin' it, you know.

"I know I can do what I want to so, it's just, you know, I want to want, and I want to be there—I want somebody to be there for me, I want it to be open. . . . I want to do this. I really don't know what it is. I don't, I don't, I really don't."

But he can always "pull it." Play the black rage thing if he needs to. Play the plaintive, caring lover, if he needs to. Be the cool dude, be the smart-ass, the dope fiend, the student. Whatever he needs to be. Be the scared man, all alone, pretending he needs no one. He's Zelig. Turning into his father.

A Green Bench

There's a faded green bench outside my father's house, its wooden arms worn thin from decades of rubbing elbows with the occupants of Shore Haven apartments. Having served its visitors so well on many Brooklyn summer evenings like this one, it now barely stands still on rain-swollen broken feet. More than a little sadness halts me in my steady step when I see it as I round the corner from the side door leaving my father's place. Like an almost forgotten friend you meet outside a store that you frequented as a child, still there, this shape makes me hesitate, out of respect for tradition, or my own fear of its secrets, I suppose. Tired, I greet it with affection. Yet I know I can't stay any longer. I make some poor excuse for my hurried parting and turn down the warm, windy street to walk three long blocks to the elevated subway stop where I catch the B train back to the Village in Manhattan.

It's a dutifully long journey on the B from Washington Square, where I stay whenever I visit New York, to the depths of Bensonhurst where my father lived for the last thirty years or so of his life. He lived in that same small apartment that I never called home until now, with his wife and two stepdaughters, until his daughters left for college or marriage or both. And there he stayed, living with his wife until two black men—a fact he could not possibly have accepted as gracefully in life as in death—took him on a stretcher to an ambulance waiting outside in the amber autumn light. They took my father for the ride of his life, with him fairly poking me in the ribs with glee about how incredibly skilled their driving was, onto the Belt Parkway through the Battery Tunnel and down the FDR Drive to a

New York University hospital in Manhattan. He died hours later after a bitter, take-no-prisoners, four-year war with a cancer that he allowed to kill him only on his own terms and according to a dictated schedule. He died on October 1, 1994.

On my infrequent and always difficult visits to him, whenever the subway passed the bridged, watery distance between Manhattan and Brooklyn, I began to struggle with the parts of me that I thought he didn't know and wondered in what place I would come to rest with his nearing death. He had been a strong, stubborn man who probably knew more about me than I cared to believe in the years when I was busy wishing he would be the father I had dreamed of.

This particular visit brought me to a father shriveled and sullen and absorbed in the endless cancer-time of his "retirement years." While Carol, my stepmother, is at work trying to store up sanity for the evening that awaits her when she returns, my father contents himself with conversations generated by his responses to whatever happens to be on the television at that particular moment. "It's all crap," he says, but he watches anyway. The television is his faithful companion, and I become the major interloper in an otherwise routinized day.

He calls Carol to confirm my arrival, turns on the radio, removes the phone from the cradle (so that would-be burglars will think that someone is at home when they call to case the joint), and we leave the building. We are headed toward "the Avenue" and the Contemporary Coffee Shop, where he has eaten nearly every morning since chemotherapy began to take away his appetite for preparing eggs in his own kitchen.

"Don't walk so fast, Kathleen; I can't go that fast." He walks slowly with a cane. It is odd for me to have to shorten my pace for this man who, all my life, had been always ahead of me, always early, waiting for me to catch up, to be on time. As we enter the coffee shop, he says, "I hope Maria's here; she's the only one who brings me my coffee right away and gets the food to the table while it's hot."

We used to joke in my family that Edward was always finished with his meal while the others were just filling their plates. He always said you were supposed to eat the food hot, insisting that if the food wasn't at the temperature of meltdown it wasn't fit for consumption. Carol, of course, complied. Now, the temperature doesn't matter. He can't really eat at all. I think he needs the familiar tocsin of hotness so that one small part of the pleasure he got from eating can still be his. If it burns his mouth, he's still alive.

Luckily, Maria is here.

"Hello, Mr. Jones." She greets him with an enormous smile and a nasal Brooklyn accent that reminds me of my younger sister's voice, already pouring the piping hot liquid that passes for coffee in Bensonhurst into a thick white porcelain mug. I rub my teeth around the mug's edges and taste the gritty familiarity of countless washings in the rack. "How are you doing?"

"Fine, fine. My daughter from California. The professor."

Maria's already shouting the order to the cook and walking toward the kitchen, leaving us alone.

"I'm thinking about applying for a job back east, Dad. It would be great to be back here again. Some friends told me about a job at the New School I might have a chance at."

"Oh, yeah? Where's Maria? I want more coffee. She's probably busy. She's the only one who can get things straight."

"It's probably very competitive, but I think I have a shot at it. I think it'd be good for Ari to be back here too, nearer his dad and his brother." I want to say, "So I'd get to see you more, too, Dad." But I don't.

Maria arrives with food and coffeepot, anticipating my father's needs.

"I'll probably hear whether I will be interviewed later in the fall."

"There's seeds on this roll. I hate seeded rolls."

Maria removes the plate, apologizes to my father, berates the cook on short order, and returns my father an unseeded roll all in one deft, seamless move. "Sorry 'bout that, Mr. Jones. Harry should know better."

"OK. It's OK, Maria. I knew it wasn't your fault."

"So, what d'ya teach in San Diego?" Maria asks me.

"She teaches political science. She teaches about all those crooks that run the government," my father says between the labored efforts of his eating.

"I teach about women and politics."

"Oh, yeah. What d'ya think about Hillary Clinton? She should just decide what her name is and keep her nose out of the president's job. I mean, we didn't elect *her,* right." Maria is excited about the subject, but my father has an opinion too.

"That moron; she's an idiot. I can't stand the whole bunch of 'em. I didn't vote for *any* of 'em. John Kennedy, Franklin Roosevelt. Now, *those* were presidents. Not this idiot. He can't do anything right."

"Well, it must be fun, what you teach. None of that when I went to college." Maria's busy pouring more coffee.

"Not when I went to college either," I add. My father pushes his plate of half-eaten food away. "Yeah, it's fun. Aren't you going to eat any more, Dad?"

"Nah. I'm done."

"Wasn't it the way you like it, Mr. Jones?"

"Fine, fine, it was great. I'm just full."

No appetite. All those poisons coursing through his veins, doing whatever, I don't know, just keeping him alive longer than anyone imagined possible. Actually, I believe that it has nothing to do with the chemotherapy—just like his death, in the end, will have nothing to do with the cancer. My father is willing his own life to continue. My father has decided he is not going to die, not yet. He wants to stick around a little longer, watch the Yankees on TV, drink some beers, see whether or not I might arrive on time for once, complain about the Russian neighbors and the lazy Arabs down the hall and the loudmouth blacks who play their music too much and too brashly for him, and hate any other group he decides to be hostile toward for awhile.

He leaves Maria a big tip.

A year and a half later, when I hear him "tee-hee-heeing this is a helluva ride" at the black ambulance driver's imitation of Mario Andretti on the Belt Parkway, I begin to imagine that my father might never have been racist after all. Maybe what it was all about was wanting to see if he could push everyone's politically correct buttons at the same time and make the whole world angry at one another and then sit back and say, "That's liberalism for you." Of course, I don't really believe that. I've seen him shout obscenities at people in public for being the people they happen to be. But what would it mean to my life if I make this subversive version of him true?

To say that we are different is to say nothing at all. The truth is, whenever I am nervously cleaning the house, or arranging the food in the freezer ("for efficiency's sake," I say), or making lists of what I need to do, need to do, I know deep in my clenched fists how very much alike we are. When he died, I found the last list of dinners that my father had planned and had pasted on the kitchen closet door as a reminder to my stepmother of the order of things. It was a list of all the foods that had been his favorites but that he had long since been unable to eat.

Sometimes, when I am folding my clothes to put them away in my dresser drawer, I remember him, the day after Christmas 1957. He is folding the clothes that were my presents that year into three neat piles in my drawer. "Now, Kathleen, you have to wait. Save these until your birthday. That's the rule." For weeks, I would open the drawer and gaze longingly at the new things, tempting but, like Sleeping Beauty, unable to be disinterred until February. This ferocious straightening things up that possesses me in times of greatest anxiety is like some ancient tribal ritual that I have learned can conjure my father's spirit. The lists that I make are a written mantra I can intone whenever I need to reincarnate the king of order and organization. Then I let it work its spell of harmony on the imagined discord of my life. And isn't that what fathers are supposed to do, put things in order?

It wasn't really that way in 1957. I was eight and my mother and father had spent all afternoon in Riley's Bar and Grill at the corner of Fifty-sixth and Ralph Avenue in Brooklyn. It was a Sunday, and the regulars had been there all day, including my parents. I remember the sickly wet smell of beer on dark wood that perfumed the cardboard coasters I used to collect to soak up the sweat from my glasses of Coca-Cola while watching my parents, drink after drink, becoming more and more loud and angry with one another for no particular reason. I knew we'd be in for one of those nights of flying statues of the Sacred Heart and the Blessed Virgin, beheaded in the fray.

Given my father's youth, lost to the need to help support his mother and siblings after his father died, and given his dashed hopes for a career in music, I suppose I can now understand the pain that he must have felt having married my mother, who hated to cook, was a slob of a housekeeper, and loved poker and booze more than she did my father. And I suppose that, given my mother's pleasure in excess—she wore the highest spiked heals and played the meanest shuffleboard I ever saw in any bar in Brooklyn—marrying my father must have taken some of the wind out of her sails. Still, since she died when she was only forty-one, and I was only twenty-one, I never got to learn as much about where she had thought she was headed as I did about my father's obsessiveness.

Later, when I was careening down my own life's highway, I used my father's obsessiveness to trump my mother's lack of boundaries and turned the steering wheel of my own crazy-car days in the right direction at the last minute. My father had done just that one Sunday night in 1957 when, screeching down Brooklyn streets on the wrong side of the road, as drunk as his wife was, with his daughter screaming in the back seat, he decided at the last possible minute to turn the steering wheel and avoid the car homing in on us at what seemed to me like ninety miles an hour. "You have to wait . . . those are the rules."

The funny thing is, I never realized until now how well suited my parents were for each other, what a sense of balance they communicated to me through extremes. No theory of codependency can unravel the tangled lives my parents wove in their disastrous marriage enough to make one clearly the perpetrator and the other simply the victim. No ideas of choice or indeterminacy can explain fully what happened to them or how or why what happened to them affected me. Every explanation leads inexorably back to some more ancient past that isn't the only one that any of us could have had because all of us have parents and ancestors who lived, and could still live, other lives.

These other lives are the stories that our parents told themselves about the lives that they were living and about the lives that they dreamed for themselves and their children. Sometimes these stories more or less matched the ones we imagined that we knew about them. Then we believed them. Sometimes these stories bore no resemblance to what we recognized as true. Then we thought our parents were deluded, and we spent years on the phone with friends, or in therapy, or with one addiction or another to figure out how their denial of the truth led to our own defensiveness or inauthenticity or bravura.

I had so many stories of my father jammed into my head at any one time, competing for the attention of my heart, that it was hard to keep them organized. My father told me stories about his life at work, about a world filled mostly with people who were not as careful as he, not as ordered as he.

He told me stories about people he knew who weren't like "the others." He knew this black man at work who was really clever, and a young woman manager who was smart as a whip. He told me about Carol's Jewish boss who really respected her, who was generous and considerate.

I listened to all his stories through different filters, depending on where

I was or what I was reading at the time of their telling. I was lucky, though, because my father would retell them and then I'd get to think about what it all meant all over again.

When I was little, my father seemed so clever, so able to fix everything. He was just like Nancy Drew's dad, always encouraging me to figure things out. Later, when I was in college and reading Marx, my father lost his job at R. H. Donnelly Company and began selling insurance in Brooklyn. So I imagined my father as a proletarian with false consciousness, another Willy Loman, another defeated shadow man like the character in Arthur Miller's *Death of a Salesman*. Once I discovered Freud, I began to worry that my father's absence from whole chunks of my life might impair my psyche. Maybe that explained why I saw him as so overwhelming a force, as someone I couldn't challenge. After feminism, I came to see my father as a man caught in the middle of several decades of confusion about what men were supposed to be. Still, he never made me feel that I couldn't be whatever I desired or dreamed up. He even did the laundry.

But though I listened carefully to all these stories, I couldn't hear in them what I wanted to hear. I really only wanted him to tell me what he thought about me, to tell me that he loved me. But he didn't share the language that I spoke. Not then.

So when he stood with me, day in and day out, during the days of the civil court trial that would determine whether I or my ex-husband would have custody of my first child, Jed, I couldn't hear him tell me, by the mere fact of his presence, that I was a good mother, a good daughter, that it was all right, that he loved me. When he paced at the end of the hall the day that I was "late" visiting him in the hospital after his heart attack— I'd come all the way from California, despite his resistance, and then, on the phone, he'd said, "Don't rush, take your time"—I couldn't hear in his impatience how excited he was to see me. When he kept the book that I had written by his side whenever he traveled, I couldn't hear him tell me how proud he was of me.

I couldn't hear him say any of these things until, in late September 1994, when I was caring for him while he lay dying, he screamed at Carol to "leave me alone, she's [Kathleen's] taking care of it" and pushed her away so that she wouldn't have to watch him disappear during the last few hours of his life. And then he pointed to the ceiling in the corner of the room, and he laughed.

"What are you laughing at, Dad?"

"You'll see."

"I don't see anything."

"Wait, you'll see . . . see that."

"See what?"

"See they're putting the meat in the truck."

"Oh, yeah."

"Did you order any?"

"No, did you?"

"Yeah. They're good, aren't they?"

"I guess so."

Then, oh, thank god, then, I heard him tell me that he loved me. And I went with him to the hospital and I stayed with him until late at night. That night, when he tried to pull the tubing out of his arms and I stopped him and he started to scream, "Help me, help, she's killing me," and then he tried to bite me and stared fiercely at me, saying, "I know what you're doing," I heard him tell me that he loved me again. He told me to leave.

All those stories haunt the present and hover on the horizon of it like some sacred talisman, some omen of the feared-for future. They are the stuff not only of novels but also of history and sociology and diplomacy. The best thing that we can hope is to tell equally good stories and to be willing to listen with humility to the stories of others. By listening, we reach past the isolation that living itself represents to connect with another, even for only a moment, and begin to believe in a world.

Stories issue, Walter Benjamin once wrote, not from a life, but its afterlife. They come out of the shadows and the rumbling sounds of the aftershock that shade and echo the life that was lived. They beckon to us, the still living, to tell about them, to talk about them, in public, in the world. A story's telling helps shape the believability of its narrative. Telling interrupts the living flux of speaking and acting and assigns meaning after the fact.

But stories are essential because they permit those moments of reflection without which action and judgment would not be possible. Because the meaning that a story assigns to an event is crafted by the storyteller, it is subject to debate and contestation. Reading it, we wonder about its meaning. We talk to each other about its effects. This does not make its narrative arbitrary, only opaque. And, that opacity serves, I believe, a political purpose: It allows us to reinsert ourselves into the narrative that is history, to become a part of the public world by participating in the process of its making. We become not only active listeners, but also, ultimately, actors and storytellers ourselves.

When I visited my father's house the next to the last time, ten months before he died, I was busy trying to collect the missing scraps of my family history. My father was a shade of pale I thought unachievable even by ghosts. He looked at me through his sunken sockets, and I felt him pulling me out of my mother's womb with his bare hands. He slithered across the floor on padded, slippered feet, making almost no sound except a low, dry cough. I noticed the crooked finger on his left hand as he tugged at my life. Has it always been so unbendable, I wondered? But I was afraid to ask. Because, for that whole day, every question that I posed was received as an insult and thrown back in my face with a silent, grimacing accusation about my own ignorance of history, family history.

"So who were the Casey's, again?" I ask, trying to grab at whatever straws remained of a genealogy.

"I told you, I don't remember. Ask Estelle, if you want to know. I don't remember that crap."

"Weren't the Casey's in the theater and arts, Edward?" It's Carol, my dear stepmother, sensing my mission and trying to help me ferret out details I so desperately crave.

"Carol, for Chris' sakes, I *don't know!* Estelle knows. What do you care about this stuff anyway."

So I get this much: Dad's Mother = Estelle Rutkowski Jones, born in Poland, claimed descendance from a "comfortable class," but worked as a seamstress for the long years after her husband's untimely death from tuberculosis. I remember her as the maker of dresses, the matriarch who ruled over a world of kielbasa, potato salad, and summers with my uncles and cousins at bright Polish carnivals filled with polkas and mazurkas in Greenpoint, Brooklyn. She was the disparaging provider of that gossamer-winged pastry known as *kruschiki,* which she baked me a mountain of, as requested, on the occasion of my first son's birth. I never met my dad's father, but I am told that Valentine Edward Jones was born in Brooklyn, New York, of Welsh immigrants. He was a barge captain, who worked the docks in Brooklyn, became a card-carrying union member, maybe even an organizer, and then some kind of political party official, probably Democratic.

The son of Valentine Edward became Edward Valentine, who played trumpet in a band from when he was eight until he was twenty-five, and left the band the year before it became American Legion national champ, the year that I was born. Edward hated unions, Democrats, liberals, welfare, blacks, the newly immigrated Russians who lived in the subsidized section of Shore Haven, and almost any other group that he could name.

Four years after Dad died, as I sat in the doctor's office, where I had been driven finally by my lover's insistence that I find out what the annoying growth spreading under the skin of my left hand was, I got another lesson in family history.

"Oh, that's Dupuytren's," said Doctor Hamer.

"It's even named after someone. Who?"

"After the person who first diagnosed it. It's associated with northern European royalty. So you can say you're descended from royalty. Usually found in men. Harder to treat in women. Unless it begins to impair your movement, unless the fingers start to curve down towards the palm and you can't straighten them out again, I'd leave it alone. Anybody in your family have this? Remember anybody with crooked fingers?"

"No."

Only later, almost by accident, when I read the notes that I had written about my visits with him and then, later still, after he died, when I dreamed about him struggling in a coffin caught in a tangled spider's web in the backyard of my San Diego house and listened to someone in my dream tell me to crush the spider so that my father could finally rest in peace, did I hear something else in my father's refusal to give me back the family history that I had wanted not to have to bury with him. All those questions that I had asked about my family history must have reminded him of his dying. If he resisted answering me, maybe his death wouldn't happen yet.

Or maybe not. I didn't get it at first, but now every time I look at the spider web under the skin of my left hand, I think about him and his tight grip. Maybe his resistance to questioning was just his old controlling self waiting even longer this time to turn the wheel to the right and finally avoid the oncoming speeding car.

Fragments of evidence, transcripts, taped reports, dreams, ghosts— these are the shards out of which I have tried to paste together glimpses of an ever-turning, ever-changing narrative. Between the lines of papers and memory's traces exist only shadows of lives. Thin-edged portraits fade into one another, a verbal Rorschach, ever open to interpretation.

And still, what do we know?

The law's judgment and psychology's categorization are two sides of the same coin. Together they create the sense that there is some path that led, almost inexorably, to that one November night. Beyond a reasonable doubt. A legal fact. A diagnostic sense of certainty. It could have been a night in my life. In yours.

Now that one November night stands out from all the rest of the nights of any year in Andrea's and Andrés's life. We search for clues to its origins in the endlessly distant past. It is so different, its end so irrevocable, that all the years before it will now and forever be seen only as a preface leading up to it. And because that night, finally, is so strange and stunningly different, it can reduce everything around it to nothing more than a rehearsal for itself. Even what came after it will be marked by its stain. Even Andrés's own death becomes an imitation of that night, a sad, undignified coda that echoes forever and unendingly the refrain of the murderous past.

I can find any number of explanations in modern psychology for why Andrés killed Andrea, for why Andrea was killed by Andrés. Manic depression, drug dependency, cocaine-induced delirium, codependency, fears of abandonment, aberrant memory function, posttraumatic stress disorder. Such explanations provide convincing reasons for what caught these two up in an intimate, violent series of U-turns that destroyed their young lives. An addict and a loser. A dedicated, motivated advocate. Someone who was sliding downward, who couldn't believe her eyes. Someone who wanted desperately to succeed, who was still strong, but who constantly blamed everyone else, even his "better self," his conscience, for his failings. Someone who would not give up, who cared too much, but not enough, just one more time. Pushing buttons, making connections.

Yet, each of these explanations misses something. Each leaves out some nuance, some suggestion of another view. With the assembled fragments of what is left of these lives, every explanation that I can find creates the idea that lives can be reduced to moments in time measured simply as cause and effect. It is this sense of certainty that I want most of all to resist.

5 Secrets

In the Shadow Houses

There's something about the shadows in Sweden. They lure you into the night. Their tranquil hue, the color of winter, lulls you, blanketing you in peaceful gray. Low-slung ceramic lamps hanging in apartment windows, hushed night-lights with just enough glow to let you see and be seen, beckon you home into the shadows. You become calm. So calm you don't notice, until it's too late to be scared, that you have been thinking about secrets.

Secrets. When I was little, I hid from the dark, all wrapped up in my blankets, even in the middle of the summer. The tiny tented corner made by my bedsheet meeting the pillow allowed enough air under the covers to last a few hours.

The dark waited for me. I knew it was there. I could hear it breathing. I knew if my toe slid out or my hand dropped off the side of the bed, the dark would grab me, pull me, drag me into the shadows, into the intimate nothingness that opened like a gaping hole under my bed. I waited for sleep. Or I watched nervously while sleep approached. Suffocating, panicked, I would finally muster enough will to call out to my mother in the middle of the night. "Please, Mom, bring me a glass of water." Oh, Holy Mother of Water, slake my thirst, bring the light. Bring the light.

The shadows are different in Sweden. Night with shadows is the longest part of the day. "You'll have a hard time adjusting to the dark," friends warn me before I leave San Diego in August. "I have never lived alone," I say. I say this out loud. I hear myself confess it like a sin. "I have never lived alone." Still, I don't think the dark will matter.

But the dark mattered a lot.

By late October, in the south of Sweden, night descends a little past three in the afternoon. I bike home in the dusk through the park. The gravelly path is a trail of frozen curves cutting close to the edge of a black river caked with ice. The cold is so sharp it has silenced my bike's warning bell and made my fingers numb. The light attached to the front wheel dimly flickers on and off. I peddle faster to make the beam stronger. Birches lining the river bank sway gracefully. Their limbs creak; they are sore from the wintry weight of snow. I want to get home quickly so I can stand on the balcony of my apartment, overlooking the train depot, and greet the last inches of night descending across the broad sky. Below me, slowly stilled railway cars gasp a little, almost unnoticeably, at the dying of the light.

I watch night come. I think about others farther north of me who have been enveloped already, nearly an hour earlier. I am jealous. Already I have learned to covet the shadows. I watch myself disappear willingly into the dark's embrace. The sun hides things you can only see at night. I burrow deeper into the seductive, enveloping gray.

Malin Ronnblom has invited me to Umeå to give a lecture. The official invitation comes from her senior professor, Gunnel Gustafson, whom I have not yet met, but with whom Malin had worked on a book about the Swedish women's movement. I take a plane from Örebro to Stockholm and transfer to another plane, landing an hour later in the Umeå airport on a quiet October afternoon.

Umeå is a smallish university town perched on the edge of the Baltic Sea in the curved arm of land that hugs the Gulf of Bothnia, two-thirds of the length of Sweden closer to the Arctic circle than Örebro, closer to the night. From its craggy coastline, Vikings set sail centuries before any of us even knew what the ocean smelled like. Malin meets me at the terminal and we drive to the Umeå Home Hotel, once the site of a hospital known for its innovative approaches to health care and now a comfortable rest stop along the eastern Swedish coast.

There are several hours before my scheduled lecture at an afternoon seminar. I long for a bath. But I content myself with the standard Swedish shower. Restless, I walk down the long halls from one end of the hotel to the other and am surprised by row upon row of cases of medical memorabilia lining the perimeter of the hotel's corridor. An odd assembly of artifacts, a museum of healing technologies and crafts. Handwritten prescriptions for homeopathic remedies rest uneasily alongside displays of steel surgical instruments of ominous proportion and intimidating function. There are implements for removing all manner of unwanted tissue, for bleeding the body of unnecessary fluids, for realigning the spirit of industrious perseverance within the most languid of souls. Or perhaps they are the engines of resignation, cool, silver devices designed to adjust one, almost painlessly, to the ordinariness, the banality, the numbing repetition of life.

Pictures of long-dead residents line the shelves. Starched-linen-apron-frocked nurses stand behind their patients, mostly women, who stare quietly into the camera, unassumingly poised, yet surprisingly indifferent to their surroundings. Did it work, I wonder? Were they called back from some deadening inertia, cured of the pains of modernity, eased out of some hungry depression, reacquainted with the possibility of love?

I take the elevator downstairs to meet Malin. We drive a short distance to the campus and join her colleagues for lunch. All during lunch I rehearse my next steps. This will be the first time that I will present this work in person in a public session. I have written about it before. I have had the words attached to the page in print, fixed in space. But it is one thing to write and another altogether to speak. I am nervous. I am worried about the response not only to my ideas, but also to that part of myself that I expose by talking about such things in public. As if on command, whole chunks of me detach themselves and line up like an army in formation, intent on providing rear-guard action against any unwelcome reception. I can now pretend that it will be easier to speak about these things here, in another country, another place, another language. But the soldiers of my spirit fail me; they fall asleep on watch, leaving me vulnerable to the fact that what I am speaking about is never so distant from anyone's life as ever to be foreign.

I begin reading the essay aloud. I have marked parts on the printed manuscript that I can choose to skip or to delete, depending on the audience, depending on my courage. I begin to sweat, having gotten to some particularly revealing part about myself. I decide, without thinking too much about it, to continue. And then my throat constricts. I think, this is silly; these are only words on a page. Yet, there it is, the repeating image of those blows, that clenched fist, that suffocating embarrassment. I finish. Silence. People shift in their seats, uncomfortable at first. I wish I could erase my words from the air and start again. Then someone opens the conversation. She asks an academic question. We all relax a bit because she has given us the opportunity to hide a little longer behind the jargon of our despair, to be comforted by the easy familiarity of our formulaic responses, to be plodding again along the familiar terrain of well-trod ideology. We breathe in the predictable airs of academic discourse. Ah, that's a relief. Please join us for the reception.

The next day, a rainy, gray day, Malin, her husband, Johan, and I and their baby, Agnes, drive out to the ancient, coastal woods just north of Umeå. Johan is an archaeologist familiar with the terrain. Along the way, we stop at a summer resort, abandoned now in the off-season's withering cold, to lunch on coffee and small sandwiches that we have brought from town. Agnes sleeps in a bundled carrier. A light rain barely mists us, but the chill is strong and when we have eaten we return quickly to the car and drive on a bit farther.

At the edge of the forest, we leave the car and travel the rest of the way to the sea on foot. Tramping across the rocky terrain to the farthest point out along the windy, austere cliffs we come to a lighthouse, a lonely sentinel still standing to warn sailors off coastal hazards. I walk ahead aimlessly, lost in thought, drawn to the sea and its mysterious, salty, familiar smells. Johan calls me back to notice the tracings of fishing and hunting encampments from the Viking age barely a few yards from the seductive pulse of the sea—-small, circular mounds of stones arranged too carefully not to be the work of our ancestors.

I stand on a pile of rocks. If you look closely, you can still see the outlines of a house that once stood there. The men's house. At special times, the women would have visited with food and drink and the warmth of their bodies to bring comfort, a lasting comfort, to the men about to leave on their long voyage. It was like that, too, among the colliers of southern Sweden. Men would have spent long winters in the woods, making coal from felled trees, cooking heavy pancakes filled with smoked bits of meat and sweetened with berry jam. Women would have brought sustenance on occasion. But winter remained the territory of men's time. So much of the ancient culture of this land has been built on a separation between men and women, a division of tasks appropriate to each, magnified by harsh, dark winters. Laws may have made this division seem irrelevant, yet it lingers, etched in stone.

The day before I visited the women's shelter in Umeå. *Kvinnohuset*—the women's house. The word's simplicity belies the complexity of its existing at all in the center of a country that so prides itself on its legislated equality that, activists have told me, it is more difficult to expose the secret of women being battered right in the middle of their egalitarian homes. Many Swedes say that men's battering women cannot exist in a country that has focused so much energy on legislating equal rights for women.

"But that is exactly the problem," Gunilla Nordenfors tells me when I interview her in the women's house on a surprisingly sunny Umeå morning. She has worked in the shelter movement for eighteen years, first as a volunteer, now as the only paid staff at one of the oldest and still most radical women's shelters in Sweden. While we talk, the phone rings insistently. Gunilla lets someone else take the calls.

"We have confronted resistance, much resistance, to talking about gender power in Sweden. Ideas about sexual equality in this country have led to the notion that if women are going to be equal then fathers have to share in parenting. Of course, we believe that fathers should play an active role in parenting. But when you have a situation of abuse of the woman by the man, there really is no way, in this society, to explain how that abuse might need to be taken into account in decisions about custody of children unless you talk about gender power.

"But, now, we have the government making new proposals to increase the role of fathers. The courts can decide to award common custody even if one parent opposes it. The courts can decide where the children should live and what the visitation rights are for the other parent. It does this in an effort to keep fathers involved. But the court does not pay attention to power divisions. So the woman becomes even more dependent on the father, has to ask him about everything, get his permission for everything. The court has reconstructed the family after divorce. Even if the woman is afraid, because of having been battered, she cannot hide because the husband has the right to know where she is, because of the children.

"The court does not understand or care about abuse. Few men are ever convicted; it's hard to prove the violence. In Umeå, in 1995, there were only twenty-two convictions and these represented only 10 percent of all cases brought by the prosecution. Only about 10 percent of the abuse cases ever get to court. And even when there are convictions, they result in minimal punishments, small fines, a few months in prison.

"ROKS, the coalition of Swedish shelters for women, has called for a tribunal on the issue of fathers' rights. It's a very sensitive issue because fathers' rights groups have been pushing very aggressively for these rights. Fathers' groups here have learned from the U.S. fathers' rights groups. What we want this tribunal to be is a place where women can talk, tell their stories, show, by witnessing, how insisting only on this legal approach to equality is dangerous for women and children."

I ask Gunilla if she thinks that this kind of critique of fathers might lead to a backlash against continuing to improve conditions for women, might even reinforce the attitude that women should bear the sole responsibility for children. She pauses to consider this.

"Whatever we do we are caught in a double bind. If we try to set up a house for women, we are criticized for being too militant, for being man haters. If we try to communicate women's stories by getting them into the media, we are accused of telling fairy tales—no, not fairy tales, ghost stories. So, we must act. We do something, but we have no control over it."

The small house in the middle of Umeå is the women's house. It is not hidden; it is on the town's map. Everyone knows how to find it. Five women "built" it by occupying it. Fifty police came to arrest the five. More women came. For three months, women slept in shifts in the building, barricading themselves into the house, keeping themselves at home, where they belonged, until they numbered one hundred. In solidarity, the one hundred women turned themselves in. One policeman was assigned to interrogate them all. Each woman confessed to some reason, some story, for her crime of staying at home, until the sheer volume of all those stories made the town give the women back the house where no men are now allowed to enter.

"Reality is something that we make every day; we see it, it helps us live. We are growing. Now, many women who call us are thinking about more than their own problems. They think about how to make change. This house reshapes the world."

"I love the shape of this logo," Britta Bjele tells me as she pauses for one moment to admire the sign on the door in the hallway outside the main entrance to the Crime Victims Bureau, a recently established clearinghouse of information about advocacy and research on crime and crime victims. We have just completed a quick tour of the small but powerful office that is housed in a renovated building on an unassuming corner of Umeå's town center. It is clear from the way her staff greets her as I am introduced to them that the respect they display in her presence is tinged with the slightest hint of anxiety that the director has just appeared in their office. Were they doing what she expected?

"Do you like it?"

"Yes," I tell her, impressed with the simplicity of the design, with the image of two clasped strong hands holding figures of people in their caring grasp, allowing them to be supported in a dignified, yet empowering, way. "I like it a lot."

"Good," Britta says and laughs a big full-hearted laugh. "I designed it myself!"

"Hej, Marianna," she says to one of her research staff walking down the hall, "come to this meeting and help me with the English."

"Of course," says Marianna, and scurries off to get some paper and the refreshments.

"It will be so much better if she joins us," she continues as we move into a lovely seminar room that she has set aside for the afternoon's meeting. "My English is a bit rough." Her English is perfect.

"Well, where shall we begin?"

Britta wears her directorial power as comfortably and elegantly as the tailored suit that gracefully announces her status. Her formidability reflects not only the fact that she leads an organization that has reshaped the ways government deals with crime victims in Sweden. It derives equally from the robust mixture of her unrestrained passion for and dedication to her work, added to the obvious pleasure she gets from letting people know, without apology, that she cares very much about her work because it improves women's lives.

What seems to please Britta most is that she has been unpredictably effective at calling attention to the extent of violence against women in Sweden. State officials commissioned a report about the scope of domestic violence, rape, and sexual assault in Sweden and asked Britta to lead the project. They thought she would do a good but ultimately bureaucratic job of it. Britta unnerved them. She laughs at the idea now, but admits there were reasons then to expect that she might have produced a quite indifferent report.

"At the time that I was asked by the minister of justice to take on the issues that I eventually reported in *Kvinnofrid* I didn't know anything about gender power. I had never experienced discrimination or any kind of sexism in my life. And the minister thought that since she and I were the same—I had been in politics, I understood it—she thought that my report would show something about the scope of the problem but would not be too radical. I would get the job done, but not make any wave—is that how you say it?" She laughs.

"But as I got into the investigation of the problem of violence against women, I learned how widespread it is. I became more radical and I knew that the report needed to be radical too. So I developed partners in the community who were thinking about the problem in the same way that I had come to think about it.

"I invited feminist researchers to talk about the issue and to educate ourselves more about how to see violence against women in a feminist way. We started by making suggestions to change the penal code. Some of these changes were radical for Sweden."

Britta hands me a copy of the 450-page report that she published under the auspicious title of *Kvinnofrid*—women's peace. "They didn't like that either, the title, I mean. They didn't like that I coined a phrase that called attention to the special circumstances that make women without peace in Sweden now, unfree in this land of equality."

Among other things, the report called for the definition of a new crime in Sweden's penal code—"breach of women's peace." This crime, the report said, "primarily involves violence and other abuses directed at women—for example spouses, cohabitants, mothers, or daughters—in close relationships with men." This was a radically new way to understand violence against women. *Kvinnofrid* demanded that the state's codification of the crime of breach of women's peace incorporate women's perspectives about the peculiar vulnerabilities that women experienced as the result of being subject to violence in their own homes. It allowed otherwise isolated hits, the individual threatening calls, to be put together into a mosaic crime—breaking the peace of women.

Adding to the controversy, the report also recommended that the Secrecy Act, passed in 1980 to protect an individual's medical and social welfare from public scrutiny, be amended to allow the public's interest in dealing with crimes of violence to take precedence over the individual's interest in integrity and confidentiality. If we don't allow health and medical authorities to report their suspicions of abuse to the state, the report said, we send a signal to the man and the woman that society does not care whether he assaults her. We must no longer allow either church or state to keep such secrets.

When a woman has been living in a relationship where she has been beaten or subject to abuse, the report continued, it is as if the specific acts themselves, the details of her abuse, fade from her memory. Like the traces of bruises, they ultimately disappear. She cannot so much remember the particular acts of abuse as she can describe the process of being terrorized in detail. "He hid my keys. He forbade me to speak to friends. He wanted his supper at a certain time. He insisted on certain foods. I wasn't wearing the right clothes. The kids were crying. He told me I am a fat, ugly pig." But these things ordinarily are not crimes; assault is a crime, unlawful threat is a crime. And without any way, in the law, to see the real crime—that the woman cannot live in peace at home—it goes unnoticed.

Kvinnofrid changes what we see. It allows us to see that breaking the peace of women may not always leave big bruises. Our ideas about crime require an abused woman to recount the details of her attacker's blows and show us her bruises. She must be able to count the times that she couldn't eat, or wished that she couldn't, and prove how he caused any of that. She must explain why she, with all her money, couldn't simply distance herself from the force of his threats, couldn't just move to another town, another world. And she must accept running or going into hiding to protect her life, or her children's lives, as the only sane choice she could have made. Anyone should know the difference between love and danger.

The deadening sound of the law's rational calculus beats rhythmically and repeatedly until it silences the memory of her earless heart's wounds. The law's measured portrait of who is right and who is wrong is so finely drawn that her eyeless mind's fuzzy image of her hurt disappears, leaving behind only the barest, whispery traces, too random to make sense.

She cannot rest, she lives in fear. Terrorized, hypervigilant, she aims to please, until the acts themselves, the clenched fists, the blows, the shouted words become part of the furniture, mere props in a domestic melodrama. Familiar, almost comforting, in their routine appearance, they signal she is still alive. Banal records of a series of individual acts the sum of which is greater that the whole, the acts themselves are the unplayed record of family secrets. Hidden in the attic, gathering dust. "No one has to know. Shhhhh. It's all right." And she can, in fact, live in such a world. Until he decides she can't. Or she decides not to. Who will get there first? Who will tell?

I met Lotte Linton in November. My friend Maria Steinberg had invited me to be part of a Thanksgiving dinner in a local church. Maria is married to an American. So is Lotte.

"There are lots of Swedish women who married Americans in the early seventies. Our Swedish-American contingent gets together every year at Thanksgiving. We like this holiday. Our kids play together, we eat turkey, and the guys watch football. We even have cranberry sauce. Can you imagine! Very American. It's fun. Maybe you want to join us?"

I say yes, wanting company, a familiar ritual, a harvest in the dark.

"So, have you enjoyed Sweden so far?" Lotte asks me in perfect English. She teaches English at the women's prison in Hinseberg.

"I love it here," I say. "I've been able to write."

"What are you writing about?" Lotte asks.

We are seated at a long table surrounded by Lotte's friends and family, and I start to tell her about Andrea and Andrés. I don't know how else to explain what I am writing except to tell their story first. I guess I keep telling the story so I can feel less alone with their memories. Yet I feel awkward talking about it. I even feel, oddly enough, a little embarrassed. Because what I am writing is both strangely public and disconcertingly private, intimate. Lotte seems to understand this. We talk for a long time before someone interrupts to ask us if we want dessert. Neither of us has eaten a thing.

"And you have gotten used to the dark?" Lotte asks.

"I don't mind it at all. In fact, I like it. I like the shadows."

December entombs me in the deep purple velvet of year's-end nights. I imagine an infinity of dark and quiet, timelessly still. I sleep late in the morning, so late that only a few hours of light remain before I am enshrouded again. Things move more slowly. I notice angles, connections between one event and another. Still awake, I watch the dark crawl into my room on cat's paws, purring at my feet, begging to be petted. I talk to the dark in dream speech, telling her my secrets. Relationships breed in hibernation; there's a long time to connect.

Lotte calls to tell me that she has arranged for me to visit the women's prison and that I will be able to interview a woman there who was imprisoned for killing her husband.

One evening, three weeks later, I am sitting in Lotte's home. She lives with her husband and three children in an old, lovingly restored, white house, set back in the woods in a town called Nora. We have just finished dinner and have moved upstairs to their quiet, very formal living room. Outside it is still snowing. The oldest daughter serves us coffee while Lotte sets out a plate of chocolates and small cakes. Her husband, Steven, and I are talking about his work with sexual-trauma victims at the hospital in Örebro. Lotte lights the candles on an ornate Victorian chandelier that hangs low from the ceiling over a long mahogany table. We are seated together at the far end of the room on a stiff red velvet sofa that is strangely very comfortable. The conversation flickers as the light mellows. We talk about Inge, trying to understand her twenty-seven-year-long marriage to abuse.

I had heard about Inge's case from Lotte and Maria before I visited the prison. It was considered unusual not only because the issue of violence against women has come to the surface in Sweden about ten years later than in the States, but also because Inge's sentence was fairly long by Swedish standards. Five to seven years in Hinseberg prison.

Earlier that day, Lotte and I had met at the turn in the road where we agreed I could park my car and drive with her the few remaining kilometers to the prison gates. Never having been to a maximum-security prison, I expected the worst: a grim, barren space filled with thick-walled Gothic architecture and heavily guarded electrified gates. As we round the last bend in the road I am surprised to see a clump of not unattractive buildings set off in a woodsy field. A secured wall surrounds the structures, some relatively new, which are grouped around an imposing central edifice raised above the rest. The manor house of what once had been a prominent farming estate, it now houses some of the inmates, the kitchen facilities, and the offices of administrative personnel. Lotte flashes her identification card and introduces me to the staff at the gate, and we enter the prison yard so quickly that I don't realize we have already passed the inspectors and been cleared.

"That's all?" I say, a stunned look on my face.

"Well, they know me and they were expecting us," Lotte answers, amused.

What unnerves me most, I guess, is that the desperate ugliness and bureaucracy of U.S. prisons, and of most state-sponsored institutional spaces in the United States, has so permeated my own expectations that I find myself disoriented, unable to stop imagining where I think I should be, almost unable to see where I am. I look for the thieves, the drug addicts, the murderers among the women bundled up against the cold, hurrying to class. They are there. I know they are.

Lotte is greeted cheerfully by some of the prisoners. They are her students, eager to see her and to meet the strange woman from the States who has come to visit them. It is a relief to be a curiosity. Since they have been studying English, we converse in broken bits of sentences, making small talk about the weather, about how far away California is from Nora, about computers. They wear casual clothes and move about relatively freely. Lotte explains that they have earned different privileges as they progress through their sentences, preparing them gradually for reentry into society. Some of them are immigrants, serving time for petty theft or for drug charges, worried about deportation. The women who have been convicted of violent crimes, a small minority, are indistinguishable from the rest, as likely as any to be learning to access the Internet or to be practicing English.

We are expected for lunch and so we enter the main building, passing down several corridors into the staff cafeteria. The fare served is typically Swedish: raw cabbage salad, boiled potatoes, some kind of boiled meat with a thick, white sauce and Jell-O for dessert. I am hungry from the cold and eat more than I expect. Eager to explain why I am visiting, I engage the guards—whom you cannot distinguish from the rest of the staff—in a conversation about their approach to incarceration and rehabilitation.

Kerstin, a former guard, is now working in a special program with women who need transition time between imprisonment and their return to freedom. She is a lively, young, attractive woman who considers herself a professional. She tells me her job is to help the women in prison see the future as one of change, of forgiveness, hope, and responsibility. Maud, her older colleague, explains that she works as a "motivator." She sees herself as someone who can help women change their consciousness. She helps them to let go of the past, not to repeat it; to forgive themselves and find a way to choose responsibility. They both tell me about the "open house" program in which they work.

"It prepares women for freedom. They have permission to leave to go to town and to take walks, and then to return. Some of them go to special groups in town, such as Alcoholics Anonymous or Narcotics Anonymous. Gradually they learn to do more for themselves. We tell them that it is their own thinking that will decide the future, whether they go back to the way things were, from one sentence to another, or take responsibility for their lives. Few decide to go back to the way things were.

"We provide special information programs for the women, to help them with special women's needs and perspectives, such as programs on women's health, abuse, on being parents. This is a new process for us, to stress motivation through information, to change consciousness. Here at Hinseberg, we provide information and motivation. For treatment programs, they go to a special treatment center or to this transitional house.

"We believe that everyone can choose information; our motivation programs are about learning how not to chose a life of drugs and alcohol. Today, we have only counseling programs, but we want to do more. We have studied an American program—"Crimes Are Like a Lifestyle"—a program started by Glen Walter, a psychologist in Fort Schuylkill Prison in New York. It was a program designed for men, but we adjusted it to Swedish culture and Kerstin modified it to fit women's needs. Women's issues are different. We try to fit our treatment program to the specific needs of each prisoner."

Kerstin has been letting Maud do most of the talking. But it is clear that she wants to share her perspective with me. I ask her how she came to this work.

"I worked for two years as a guard. I was good at what I did. I had a rapport with the prisoners. My bosses saw that I was good. But I wanted to do more. I believe that people can change if we help them. So I asked to be sent for more training. When I came back, I started up the special group meetings for the women. We had to fight to get them organized, but the women bosses supported us. They said, 'Go for it!'"

"We have to go for it," Maud adds, "because we are women."

"I plan to go back the university," Kerstin continues, "to get my certification as a drug counselor. I want to expand this program."

They leave, so that I will have time to talk with Inge.

When Inge enters the room, I am struck at once by the odd fact that she is both a small and big woman—broad shouldered, with petite facial features, short ash-blond hair, and thick hands. She sits down at the table and Lotte introduces us. Her wide smile disarms me. As she tells her story, her life fills the room. She talks to me through Lotte's translation. Some of the Swedish I can understand after the four months I have lived in Örebro. And Inge can understand some English. But the language that we are speaking has no fixed boundaries. It has a grammar and a logic, a syntax of its own. It reaches past geography and history to carry a story that could have been about anyone at any time in any place. The story means something different every time it is told; it has its own peculiar nuances; it is all too familiar.

The psychological abuse was worse than the physical abuse, Inge says. It was easier to be beaten, she tells me, than to feel worthless, to be called a useless piece of trash, a fat slob, a nothing.

"I stayed," she says, "because I felt at least that was a life I could control. If I left I would have to hide out in a women's house or tell someone what was happening. Some people thought they knew. But I never said anything. I didn't dare. No one wanted to interfere.

"One day I decided I needed to do something to him. Make him stop. Make him stop. I felt like I was two people, one saying, Yes, do it, and the other saying, No! Don't! But I had to do this. I don't know what I was thinking. I reached a limit. Everyone has a limit. You know, this is where it stops. You need to cross a line to want to make it stop.

"My two-year-old grandchild was staying with me that night and I didn't want him to wake up. So I made sure he wouldn't hear anything. I asked my son to show me how and I loaded the gun. He was fifteen. He heard the shot. He said to me, 'Now he can't hurt us any more.' He understood, this had to happen. It was not directly planned, but it had to happen. Then I buried him in the yard.

"And then, now, maybe you will think this is sick, but then I went to the store and bought food for me and my son. We ate. For the first time, we ate what we wanted.

"I felt like I had saved my son's life and my own. He had always threatened us, beat the kids, showed me the gun he was going to use to kill me with. When he was dead, no one even noticed that he was gone. His mother called, but I told her that we had had a fight and then he had left. I told my daughter-in-law the same story. But she didn't believe me. So I told her the truth. She said, you must tell the police. I said, yes, I will, but first my younger son and I are having a vacation. Then I waited. My daughter-in-law finally said, if you don't go to the police I will. So I told them what I had done. By then, it was nearly three years after the murder.

"The worst thing of all, the worst punishment of all, was knowing I had killed him and carrying that around all alone, without confessing, for three years. Only when they put me in jail, after three years, did I realize I had done a crime.

"In court, the prosecutor asked me, why didn't I divorce. He didn't understand my dilemma. I tried to explain. I did take the law into my own hands. I didn't want to excuse the crime. It was wrong what I did. But I wanted to explain the situation. I felt like I was saving my own life, my son's life.

"But the guilt that I feel is as much for putting my children into that situation as for killing him. As a woman, I wanted to get away, but I cared, I cared. I was torn. I must have cared for him deeply, anyway, unconsciously, I liked him but really I felt like I hated him. I was weak because I let this happen. But others say that's how it works; others here at prison have experienced the same thing and ended it the same way.

"I used to think that it was just here, with us in prison. Then, when you see all the others, you see it's one after the other who have experienced the same thing, you know that it's a situation. You're not alone. Sharing the many things we have in common is important, so you can change.

Then Inge pauses to tell me one more thing. "I have had a major change in my life. An old classmate of mine, a man, looked me up after he saw the story about the murder on the television show. I was never going to look at another man again. But this short, skinny, bald-headed man with the big heart, he would take down the moon for me.

"Still, I dream about what happened all the time. I dream that I have just moved into a big house with many things; my son is seven or eight; there are many things to clean and not enough time. I am stressed for time and I cannot do anything. I am still afraid."

Sentence by sentence, in the rhythmic lilt of a hypnotic Swedish ronda, embellishing each repetition with more detailed, elaborate chords, Inge has recounted her life. We have been sitting together for more than an hour. And then I notice that none of us has minded the fact that the room is almost completely dark. Even when Inge got up to use the restroom, she returned without putting on the light. It has felt disquietingly comfortable for the three of us women to be sitting alone in a darkening room listening to one of us telling the others about how she murdered her husband.

As Inge talked, I watched her grow before my eyes. I try to explain to her what her words have made me see. I tell her that she has made me feel what she felt so much that I can see how coiled up and small she must have been before and I can also see how big she has become now. I tell her I can see her cowering. I can also feel her strength. But I cannot feel her anger. She must have killed out of fear.

"I see how strong you are inside here," I say, gesturing to my heart.

She is surprised, embarrassed. "Inside here?" she says. Meaning inside the prison.

"No, inside *here*," I say, gesturing again.

"I am still afraid," she says. "I have lived inside here for so long that I am afraid of leaving. I feel so safe in here," Inge says. "I have never felt so secure. I have my routines. I need to keep them. I am afraid of the openness, of the freedom."

Lotte and I leave. The snow is a thick down blanket, heavier than all winter. We walk silently toward the car. I glance back at the walls of the prison and wonder how we will ever get home.

But we just go there; we just go home.

Who Knows What?

Before I left for Sweden, while I was still in my routines, it was easier to hide. Too busy at work, too distracted by the university, too comfortable at home, there is too much else to do. Can't sleep. Can't write now. But, even in the fall when I took leave from work and came to Sweden to write and to research, I noticed that I could still spend whole chunks of time avoiding the point of the story. I sought old friends on the Internet, looking for someone to talk with, to talk about what I was writing.

To talk about it, not to write it. Hiding again, looking for someone who might be awake in the middle of the night, needing to talk.

Then one night, a friend writes to me.

"Hey, it's been a long time, hasn't it, Kathy. I've been meaning to write and I keep putting it off. How are you? Where are you? What are you doing? Liz and I moved to Iowa! Can you believe it! *Iowa.* But we love it here and things are going well. I finally have a real tenure-track job and the department here is great. How are you?"

I am so thrilled to hear how well things are going with my friend. I write her about everything I have been thinking and doing. I tell her about my news. I tell her it is so strange to be alone in another country. I tell her about the writing. About being alone. About the story.

She thinks I am writing about a student we used to know at Berkeley.

"Is the student you are writing about Daria? I had her in a class, too, and went to a memorial service for her after she was killed. Or is there still *another* women's studies student who's been killed by her boyfriend?"

"Oh my god, I forgot all about Daria! I don't think I had her in class when I was teaching at Berkeley, but I remember, now that you mention it, the rough outlines of the whole thing. I am going to want to talk to you about this more, later.

"Yes, this is *another* student, an SDSU student who was the head of the student-run women's resource center and who was murdered in 1994. Andrea O'Donnell. I knew her very well. . . . When was Daria killed? Do you have material, I mean newspapers, from that time? Would you be willing to be interviewed about this? Know others who would be? It would only form a part of what I am doing, but I am writing about how we talk about 'choice' . . . that we have tended to set up these 'unreasonable choices' between love and power, and the 'we' in this case is the general culture but also feminism in connection to the covering over of the complexity of the truths of our lives. I mean, I think we keep secrets about how really difficult it all is. This is . . . a challenge. . . . Well, anyway, if willing to continue to talk, would love to."

I try to picture Daria but I cannot remember her very well. I write to another friend of mine, a former student who was in that fall class that I taught on women and politics the year that Andrea was killed. Susan is now living in Berkeley. She agrees to help find some articles on Daria, to search the newspapers and help me make a few contacts with some folks who might remember Daria.

A thirty-year-old undergraduate majoring in sociology at UC-Berkeley and working as a lab assistant in a plant research center on campus, Daria Aponte was killed on August 28, 1991. She was found in her boyfriend's bedroom, naked and bleeding from a gunshot wound to the neck, when police responded to an early morning 911 call to Niccolo Janelli's house in the Berkeley Hills. Naked himself, Niccolo apparently had been trying to stop the flow of blood from Daria's neck before he called the police. He claimed Daria had pulled the trigger.

Daria died less than an hour after she was taken to Alta Bates Hospital in Oakland.

The coroner ruled her death a homicide, meaning, literally, death at the hands of another.

Daria was well known in the women's studies department at Berkeley. Yes, she had had intimate relationships with women. People knew about that. She wanted to go to medical school and work on women's health issues. People knew about that too. But she didn't talk much about her boyfriend, Niccolo, whom she had been dating for only three weeks. "Something just doesn't add up at all," friends said.

Two weeks later campus groups held a memorial service to honor Daria Aponte. Niccolo Janelli showed up to grieve after most of the mourners had left.

"I wasn't told about the service because they figured it would be a very bad scene," he told reporters. "A lot of details haven't come out. Everyone that knows me knows what happened. I hope some day it becomes all more clear. Everybody is extremely destroyed that it has happened."

Threatening his life if he stayed, another friend of Daria's told Niccolo to leave the scene.

In May 1992, Niccolo Janelli pled guilty to involuntary manslaughter. Nearly a year after Daria's death, after investigations and delays in court, he was sentenced on August 20, 1992, to serve two years in state prison for the accidental killing of his girlfriend, Daria Aponte. Niccolo's friends thought that the sentencing was excessive. Daria's friends thought that he had gotten away with murder.

It was Deputy District Attorney Jack Radisch of Alameda County who had decided to press charges against Niccolo Janelli. "I believe he pulled the trigger — it was practically physiologically impossible for her to fire the gun. He's down there between her legs with the gun pointing at her face pulling the trigger. We call that gross negligence. And that is a crime."

Radisch contended that the circumstances at the scene at the time of death indicated that the couple was acting out a dangerous sexual fantasy.

Daria's friends thought that such stories were sensational. They were just convenient ways to ignore Niccolo's rage against Daria. She wouldn't have been involved in that kind of fantasy, they said. She would have known better. She was very interested in women's issues and health care issues. She was a very determined, strong-willed person. Besides, Nicco was the only person in the house with Daria at the time of the shooting.

Now isn't that convenient, Daria's friends said. He'll get away with killing her. He's probably got a fancy lawyer who'll get him off the hook. He'll get away with it.

"He's a sweet guy and he wouldn't have hurt a fly. He would never have deliberately hurt anybody," said Nicco's friends.

"He's a dangerous, scary man," said Daria's friends.

"I would trust him with my life," said Nicco's friends.

"It was an accident," said Nicco's father. "It could have been avoided."

"We don't really know what happened. The only people that would know are people who were there. One's dead and one's alive," said the deputy D.A.

We can't find malice or motive, the district attorney's office said. But we know she didn't shoot herself.

Inge and Daria and Andrea. Are they all unexceptional cases of abuse? Or is there something more that they have in common? Is what they have in common the simple fact that they kept their own women's secrets, that they stopped themselves from shouting down the world?

Minerva's Owl

I have to admit that dealing with the fact of Andrea's death in the middle of a women's studies department made me stop and think about what kinds of secrets any of us may have kept, knowingly or not. What kinds of wisdom have we hidden from ourselves that, if leaked, might make us all shudder a little about how we should have known better? I believe in the owl of Minerva, that philosophical harbinger of wisdom. The trouble is she follows always a little too late after the fact. So we probably could not have known how our belief that choice was an empowering, intoxicating elixir might confront us one day with a paradox or two, might grab us right in the middle of its bittersweet grip, right in the middle of our lives.

When I first got to San Diego State, I wondered about the history of the place. The women's studies department was in the middle of its ten-year review, so it seemed natural to wonder about the past. I had heard about the legacy of the department's early split, different stories about the rancor between the purist revolutionaries, who wanted feminist ideological cleanness at almost any price, and the compromising institution builders, the pragmatists, who wanted security at almost any price. Institution building prevailed, but with the ironic consequence that everyone who had been teaching in the original curriculum left. The revolutionaries and the pragmatists, self-outcasts or cast out before the administration found the resources to create an official department of women's studies, were all gone, dispersed, by the time that I arrived. New faculty had been recruited for the new program.

Several of the exiled activists went on to form the Center for Women's Studies and Services (CWSS), a storefront operation in downtown San Diego that offered a nontraditional, nonacademic setting for radical and socialist approaches to feminism. In 1980, the year I arrived in San Diego, CWSS was still very actively providing classes in basic feminism and consciousness raising in its off-campus location. It also was becoming a community leader in rape crisis intervention and in educating the police about the importance of incorporating women's perspectives on sexual violence into their training and intervention programs. The department dutifully advertised CWSS programs. But a rift had been created between the two groups that only many more years of separation might begin to heal.

I felt that rift echo in Andrea's life and death. It certainly had fashioned departmental mythologies and re-created patterns of ideas about women's studies' past and future that spread out beyond us and attracted to us certain students who were seeking different ways to make sense of their lives.

By mythologies I don't mean lies. I mean the kinds of stories we tell ourselves about who we are and what our purpose in life is or should be. Mythologies are the tales that faculty and students share, or are divided by, over the years. One constant theme we have held onto is the idea that women's studies could be a different kind of place within the academic institution in which it existed. We felt that women's studies would become a safe haven, an island in the male-stream, a promised land, a resting place, a locale of sinister wisdom and sisterly support.

But the place we all were willingly entering had a self-legitimating appeal whose powers we may not have fully considered. The high stakes of tenure and promotion meant that anyone who got to stay had to prove herself according to the ordinary rules of the credentials game. This game made it risky to feature political activism prominently, even in women's studies. We couldn't choose to push any political agenda too hard without threatening our own right to exist within the confines of the university. That's how it felt then and still does.

So we modified our mythology to fit the system. We would be different, we said, not because we were less scholarly, but because the focus of our scholarship was different, because our faculty were feminists and our research reflected women-centered values. And, we argued, those differences would constitute something like a revolution within. Women's studies would give us a powerful base. Women would feel comfortable and respected in our territory. Their voices would be heard; their experiences would be viewed as a credible source of knowledge. Women's studies would be a zone of safety for women, an academic home.

Minerva's owl. I guess I wonder now, in hindsight, what kinds of principles we may have unwittingly endorsed to establish this zone of safety around ourselves. I don't really think we could have known, under the circumstances, how much our choice of scholarship, of intellectualism, would require us to continue to keep our distance from activism, from politics, at the very moment when our curriculum was promising that we would change the world.

At the very moment we were promising to change the world, we were becoming more aware that the university system demanded adjustments and that professionalism required standards of performance that might limit our efforts. But by then, we already were living in a changed economy.

In the early eighties women were just beginning to arrive on the academic scene in noticeable numbers. Even though we were few, the system acted as if there were still too many of us trying to cram ourselves into the tiny box of academia, into the too few places that were willing to hire us. Newly minted Ph.D.s in hand, we were being squeezed by the growing fiscal crisis of the state on one side, and a professoriat not yet ready for their golden years on another side. On still another side, add an alive and functioning old boys' network of chums who were comfortably tied to their alma maters and unwilling to cut the cord. Then, on the fourth side, watch us close the door tightly behind ourselves while heeding the call for feminist careerists, barely noticing the warnings about what might happen to us inside the space of male careers.

Living in such close quarters within the context of a university not altogether welcoming to feminists, coupled with the open-ended and consciousness-raised expectations of students who found their way into our classes, contributed to women's studies becoming a self-policed enclave. Self-contained and safe. Yet, ironically, under these circumstances, we were also more vulnerable to criticisms or scandals internally or externally generated. The balance between feminism and the academy was so precarious that we needed to be extra careful not to make mistakes. If one of us slipped up, we would all be damaged. So we guarded our own small territory of legitimacy, wary of the criticism of legions who would have preferred—and still do prefer—that we not exist at all.

The easy criticism to make is that women's studies created the same kinds of exclusions that it had criticized in others. But that's not my point. I think we assumed, a little too simply, that we could create a place where every woman who sought it would find what she wanted or needed. If we didn't assume this, maybe we simply allowed that illusion of safety to go a little too unchecked or unmodified. In any case, we weren't really prepared for the fact that creating safe spaces came with a price. Becoming a guardian in a house of safety can come at the cost of feeling you have to be perfect. And the pressure of perfection can make you feel that there can't be anything dangerous or out of kilter about the ways you are living your life. Right in the middle of the safe house of feminism, it's possible to feel all alone and without protection.

But all this is hindsight. My own private year of living dangerously was 1980. I arrived in California, out of a job and out of focus in a place of endless sun, easy cheerfulness, and the odd cultural practice of greeting strangers with more "Have a nice days" and apologies for the rain than I had imagined was humanly possible. It was an awkward time for me. There were few reasons I could give, without wincing, to explain why I had left Wilmington, North Carolina, and moved to San Diego, California, at just about the worst time in decades for any academic seeking employment in her profession. Wilmington wasn't exactly a thriving megalopolis that urbane professionals were falling all over themselves to get to. But at least I had a secure job there. And there were far fewer such university jobs every day. Why did I leave?

That question, to a feminist in the early eighties, was the proverbially loaded one. I didn't think that I could say, without sacrificing my women's lib credentials, my seriousness as an academic, my foot in the door, and the possibility of a future in one place forever, amen, that the reason I left Wilmington and sought the sunny south of California was to try to save my marriage. But that, in fact, was the truth. Or a good part of it.

Had you known me then you would have seen the young feminist activist, the rebellious academic unafraid intellectually to stand up to the combined forces of patriarchy and capitalism in public. You might never have guessed, from my public persona, that I was finding it increasingly difficult to sleep and breathe at the same time. Nothing was working the way it was supposed to. My marriage was coming unglued. Yet my kids needed stability. So I kept the family intact, even though I found it difficult to believe that stability led to happiness by some inexorable law of the universe. I loved my husband, my kids, and my job. It was a ménage à trois, an impossible equation to balance. Stay or resign, the North Carolina dean had said. One less thing to work on. For now. And I resigned.

But I didn't give up entirely. Maybe, I thought, it would be a good idea to seek the guidance of an older, wiser woman. Just in case. So I called Betty Nesvold, one of the founding mothers of the Women's Caucus of the American Political Science Association, and then chair of the Department of Political Science at SDSU. Betty was an SDSU grad who had decided, later in her life, to follow her dreams. She moved her family to the North American tundra—Minnesota—and, while raising her five kids along with keeping her marriage intact, earned her doctorate in political science from the University of Minnesota. Luck of the draw. To me, Betty wasn't someone who had everything so much as she was someone who had tried to keep her life whole. So I wrote to her.

"This is probably just about the worst time to be looking for a job, Kathy. California is swimming in unemployed Ph.D.s." She wasn't discouraging, just pragmatic. "But when you get here, call me. We'll go to lunch."

I'll never forget the day that I met Betty at the Faculty Staff Center on campus for lunch. I arrived at the lunch having moved beyond nervous to calmly paranoid. I didn't know where I was going and I was sure that there were folks following me. As we walked through the line, pushing our trays along the slippery surface in front of one of about a thousand look-alike salad, soup, and sandwich bars—the signature cuisine of California—I was mentally rehearsing my self-promotional speech, not noticing that the strap of my purse was teetering dangerously off-angle on the edge of my shoulder. We moved toward the table, my purse moved toward my elbow, and the soup of the day collided with the half-sandwich special, smashing the whole mess on the floor. Betty looked up at me, and in her inimitable deadpan way said, "You know, Kathy, they say that first impressions are lasting ones."

A week later the department called to offer me a couple of courses in women's studies, and I started teaching at SDSU in spring 1981.

I settled easily enough into the department's rhythms. There was no identifiable party line; some of the faculty were more socialist leaning, others more radical feminists. Each of us had a disciplinary specialty and our curriculum tended to follow these specialties. I taught a course called "Sex, Power, and Politics" and remember, with amusement, the irate response of one of my early students. He harrumphed out of the class when he learned that our focus was not on the affairs and forlorn love lives of members of Congress—many of whom were very much in the news at the time—but instead on the ways that women's second-class political status had been created right in the middle of democratic traditions.

Most of the faculty with whom I worked then still are working at SDSU now. A few have left, gone on to other academic positions or even other professions. Some of them stay in touch. I hear about one or two others through the long-distance network of rumors and half-facts, of implication and innuendo and an occasional confirmed sighting, that sends images of word and deed about successes and failures along the wireless perimeters of the academic surfaces of our lives.

There is another group, a group of faculty who preceded me and many of my colleagues by a few years. They are the "early ones," the set of folks who created the department in 1970. We hear about them through the grapevine of activists and community workers who are their colleagues now and who keep us informed about the still significant kinds of world-building activities with which many of them have been, and are still, meaningfully engaged. They have their successes and failures too.

I thought about all these women—those who stayed and those who left—when Andrea died. And then I remembered that this was not the first time that we had had to confront secrets. I remembered that, nearly a dozen years or so before Andrea's story, none of us had noticed until it was almost too late that one of our own colleagues, "Dr. C," was being beaten in her own home by her woman lover, "F," an adult SDSU student who had taken a number of women's studies classes.

I write to Dr. C. "It's been a million years since we have been in contact. . . . I am writing to you now to see if you are interested in helping with a project." I am not sure what I expect. I tell her about Andrea; that I am trying to write about the question of how we think and act and talk about choice in women's lives; that I want to generate thinking about these issues, get us all talking again about the complexity of our lives. I tell her that Andrea was the head of the Women's Resource Center on campus. I ask her if she would be willing to be interviewed. I think it will be important, I say, if she shares her story, her experience with violence. "This is difficult to put in a letter, but I think your story—and the story of others of us who consider ourselves feminists and yet have had great difficulty in times in our life negotiating the balance between power and love—can make a difference to the ongoing public debate about these issues." I let her know how to contact me. We might be able to meet in the fall, when I will be in her town for a conference, I suggest. I wish her well.

But the letter is returned to me stamped "Addressee Unknown." I am disappointed, but not discouraged. I find another address for her and try again.

Chance or fate, take your pick, but something allowed me to retrace the unmarked steps she took to get as far away, in spirit and geography, from San Diego as she could.

And now we are talking on the phone.

She says she hardly remembers me. "But then there is so much that I try not to remember." She says she'd be willing to meet and talk. It will be part of the work she finds she still has to do to heal, to feel whole. It's been a long process, she says. "But before we meet, I'd be interested to see how you are going to approach this. Can you give me some clearer idea of what your perspective is?"

I find it difficult to explain. So I begin with Andrea's story and where that has led me.

"Maybe it's easier if I send you some of what I have already written," I finally say. "Then you'll have a better idea of where I am trying to take the discussion."

"Fine. And I can send you something that I wrote too; something that I wrote about what happened to me."

"That would be great."

It had been written nearly ten years ago, several years after the blows had stopped. I read Dr. C's recounting of the pain of having been a woman battered by another woman. "Much of what happened I have veiled over and forgotten, hidden in shame." She remembers that the blows taught her something about physiology. A blow to the head makes your eyes blacken. The fear of being discovered pushes you to despair, drives a wedge in your heart, makes you feel dirty, ashamed, responsible, makes you feel weird, friendless, invisible. Makes you hide out in the middle of the day, walking down the halls of the university, not audaciously, but blindly, bare bruised arms exposed, expecting no one to notice. And, obligingly, none of us did. At least, no one admitted to it then. Not until it was almost too late, but luckily, Dr. C says, just in time. "A colleague saw the bruises on my arms. . . . I came up with the old saw about having walked into a door. She did not believe it." Then someone did see her exhaustion and disorientation and, calling her bluff, helped her find a way out. With her life, but not with tenure, intact. Well, there are standards, after all. And it's safer if she goes away.

Later that summer, we begin to correspond. She shares with me her thoughts about her own writing, her effort to write herself free of the past by incorporating it into her present. It brings her to the question of power, she says. There was so much in that earlier time in women's studies where we thought we could rid the world of power, erase the vestiges of its structures from the world. She is reminded of those times when she thinks about what happened to her. We thought we could wish away hierarchies, she says. She says that even she thought that then. But it's a lie.

Trying to wish away power is a lie. We need it. In fact, the world is more dangerous when you pretend that power is not, or should not be, part of life, she says. Her work now has meant that she has had to own her power, acknowledge it, come clean with the times in the past when she may have misused it. Or, rather, she says, there were times when she was in a nominal position of power and may have failed to take it up. Failing to take it up meant that she failed in her responsibility to use her power. With F, that was certainly the case, she says. Perhaps that is what let her, Dr. C, be open to her own abuse. Yet in the eyes of the harshest of critics, it was she who violated the boundaries with F. After all, F had been her student. That's true, she says. "Yet, just as clearly, I was also a victim. These things are maddeningly complex."

Power. So much more complex than any of us imagined. Where is the boundary of abuse? Neither the use of "consent" nor its simple rejection gets us very far, whether we are talking about rape, sexual violence, harassment, or abuse. But neither does the invocation, the simple invocation, of power. Yes, you may have ostensibly had power, I say, but so does the one who seems to be the victim. We don't want to touch this very often, I say, because we want to understand how, for instance, F's prior history explains why she may have behaved the way that she did. But so may yours. And then we are left with nothing, since we all have histories that can explain away the present.

Isolated, embarrassed, cut off from her colleagues. In the end, they helped her escape. But, she says, there is more than a little irony in a women's studies faculty member's being a domestic violence sufferer right in the heartland of feminism.

I don't find it so surprising anymore that any of us are having these sorts of things to deal with, I say. So many of us have had similar problems. But I think that we have been afraid to articulate this in a way that would add complexity to our thinking. And so we are left with a certain ideological fixity, even disingenuousness. Not everyone does this. But I do think many of us fall "victim" to the assumption that our ideas will set us free.

This assumption can make you feel isolated, like you felt, I tell her. It added to Andrea's isolation, I think. Perhaps she couldn't tell any one of us that she was having the kinds of problems that she was having because, after all, she was a feminist and none of this was supposed to be happening to her. And she was a survivor; she could take care of herself, solve any problem herself.

"Yes, maddeningly complex. We will talk."

We arrange to meet when I will be attending a professional conference in a city near where she now lives.

As I get off the elevator and walk into the lobby, I recognize her almost immediately. Then something reminds me of a nearly forgotten image of her hidden in the recess of my mind for years. I remember one day long ago, no day in particular. She was sitting in her office, wearing an almost forlorn look, saying nothing, staring into space, her long hair dragging her face down. I never asked her then what was the matter. Instead I carried that stillborn picture of her in my head like some fragile ghost of the person she had wanted to become. I carried it until the minute she turned to greet me and I see that I was always fooled. For years I had been caught in that wrinkle of time where your mind lets your soul slip back from responsibility and into that sickening quagmire of regret and pity.

Now I see who she is, always was. Her posture shows a steady peacefulness, the strength of kindness that supports the person she has become—someone who has settled into and forgiven herself.

She had written: "Only now, much time and therapy and other experiences later, do I feel ready to both fully accept this as part of my life and to begin to let it go."

And I can only think about the accidents and memories that have taken us this far. How much easier it would have been to continue to push past each other in the halls of life, each immersed in her own private anguish, innocently unaware of the other. Silently, we might have decided to remain the walking wounded, lost, forever alone. Instead, she reaches out her hand and shakes mine, and smiling, says hello. We walk to the elevator and take it up to my room.

"Would you like something cold to drink?"

"Yes, thanks," she says, settling into a chair near the table at the far end of the room. We have decided to talk here because she feels more comfortable with the privacy it affords. She is not so much worried about meeting anyone that she knows than that we will be interrupted.

She tells me she has been thinking about how lucky she was that she escaped with her life.

"I think the most important message of fact that I have learned from your analysis," she says as we are beginning to talk about her story, "is that I didn't look like a 'typical' victim. Maybe the distancing I felt—because I didn't look like a victim, and really who does—was because any one of them [in women's studies] knew that she could have been there, where I was; maybe that was what led to the distancing and the unfriendly reception that I got from them.

"Resilience? I guess I had that. But what explains it? What makes the difference between one person's survival and another's disappearance? I think asking how one can survive is a hope-generating question.

"I know now that I was trapped by secret keeping. The woman with whom I had been involved, who became my abuser, also had been my student. Never mind that we were close in age. Never mind that I had originally befriended her to support her through a rough time, and later housed her when she lost her apartment. Never mind that she pursued me for well over a year before we became lovers. Despite all that, I knew that it was inappropriate, a boundary violation. But I was not capable of maintaining boundaries at the time. I have now generated the harshest of criticisms of the situation. I still have problems, still struggle with that, still ask, after all these years, how could I have done that. And all I can say is: one bad decision, motivated by what seemed like compassion but in the end showed itself also to be fear—it was one bad decision at a time.

"I know that I was lonely in San Diego. Why wasn't the place congenial to me? Partly because I had no other colleagues in my field. I guess it just never came together for me. And so much of it was shot through with what happened to me, what happened with F.

"I can find all sorts of reasons why it happened. Some of the counter-cultural norms at the time might have contributed to the ease with which I seemed to have let myself fall into that situation. I also thought then that I could make a difference in F's life. I thought that I was providing posi-tive energy, helping her get herself together. I know now that this led me to engage in conversation in ways inappropriate to my role, to talk about things beyond my skills to handle and inappropriate in the context.

"F fit the profile—she had been raped, been in a violent marriage, been an incest survivor. She played the victim role well, played on my own guilt about my relatively privileged life. She played on my weaknesses. I had money, the status of a 'professional.' Yet, none of this protected me from being vulnerable to her blackmail power.

"She was able to appeal to my own sense of 'ethics.' I held to the idea that I was a kind person. I would have had to become a mean, horrible person to throw her out of my house or call the police when the violence started. It was the 'love and care' piece that kept me there, got me to allow things to happen.

"At the time, there was so much thinking about egalitarianism in women's studies. F had that ideology of 'we're all equal in struggle.' I was buying it partially, or at least being silenced by it. So I allowed her to stay in my office even during conferences with other students.

"Of course, the chair of the department sent a memo telling me that I could not allow people to sit in my office like that. At the time, she had no idea what was really going on in my life. The memo seemed appropriate to me. I had let the boundaries slip. But F hit the ceiling—she screamed about elitism. And it provoked the first of two of the most serious pieces of violence. I allowed her to stay; she pretended to be helpful.

"The very elements that isolated me from everyone meant that I could not, would not, seek help. There was the 'ethics' factor again—she was a student. I was embarrassed by the situation I found myself in; trapped, afraid to ask for help, hamstrung by the very idea of power that she always reminded me that I had had and she lacked. But, just like Andrea, all the power that I had was rendered completely unavailable to me by the intensity of her violent rage. And my own embarrassment.

"How did what was really happening all come out? Another women's studies colleague saw my bruises; she wouldn't listen to my excuses. She reported it to the chair. And the chair worked out a plan for my escape with the head of Counseling Services. F was in my office when I got the call from counseling that she had to see me right away. Something let me make some excuse to F about needing to go to an appointment. And the chair and the counselor laid out their plan. I was in trouble, in danger. I needed to leave. Immediately. My classes would be covered. At first I protested, and then I said yes.

"I stayed with the department chair that night. I called my folks and explained why I was coming home. I took with me what I could carry on the plane. And I left.

"The tenure process was still going on. So, when it came to its predictable end, I got to read a several-pages-long, single-spaced document about my various academic shortcomings from the same folks who had saved my life. That I knew I hadn't been doing my job very well for some time did not make this any easier."

She knows there is nothing clear-cut about what happened. She knows she survived. She feels grateful to her colleagues for helping her. Still, she wonders about the irony of it all. She would have been a very unpleasant reminder of a very unpleasant, nearly uncontainable, incident if she had figured out how to stay. Or even if, after a semester away, she had been able to come back to complete what academics call a "terminal" year, a professional safety net provided to break the fall of those whose scholarly or teaching performance is not up to par.

"San Diego State University has the oldest women's studies department in the country." I cannot count the number of times I have uttered that phrase. In the right kind of crowd, it still gets a lot of oohs and aahs.

There is a peculiar weightiness that surrounds the body and soul of an elder. The weightiness is the heaviness of responsibility. Being the eldest department leading an academic revolution is no exception. People watch what you do and decide to follow or to take another path.

Recently, the responsibility of the eldest women's studies department has become more complicated. The significant and growing media industry, attentive to every quiver of public criticism of women's studies and feminism, hasn't made anyone's job in women's studies easier. Criticism of women's studies in influential popular magazines and newspapers, on television and radio, as well as in books, has been lauded by the *New York Times,* the *Washington Post,* and the *Wall Street Journal* as brave and innovative. The critics get featured in glossy-magazine cover stories, in glamorous poses, and on talk radio and almost-ready-for-prime-time television shows.

Sometimes I think that this degree of criticism should be taken as a compliment, an unequivocally positive measure of our success. You don't bother to criticize something that has no institutional power. At other times I think that we have needed the criticism, and should have even more of it, in order to stay honest and to remind ourselves of the responsibility that comes with the territory of influence. Having been legitimate and successful in academia for this long, we should be able to survive a few sideswipes. Despite our bickering with conservative women who bemoan the lack of evidence solid enough to quantify once and for all the real power of patriarchy, and our disgruntlement with feminist socialist radicals who recant their revolutionary ways, maybe we should recognize that these critics have given us an important opportunity to be self-reflective. We have grown with other critiques; why not with these too? What opportunity would we be missing if we act too defensively in response to the latest barrage?

It may be true that the amount of media attention doled out to the detractors of feminism has been directly proportionate to the amount of media *in*attention that usually surrounds solid feminist scholarship. Criticisms of feminism, especially by former practitioners, make for dramatic stories.

Yet I think there are other, more complicated and compelling, reasons why the rhetoric attacking feminism resonates and circulates in so many quarters. Accusations that feminists simplify problems, such as domestic violence, and villify institutions, such as the family, in the interests of ideology speak to an unease that each of us has felt. If we are honest enough to admit it, some incident has made each of us uncertain about feminism's ability to offer simple, pragmatic solutions to complex problems. Even though this unease is not the fault of feminism, we haven't dealt with it very well. It's been too unsettling. We haven't gone public with our unease. We cover; we say that we never implied feminism was simple. We are, frankly, frightened of our own vulnerability. I am, anyway.

So when critics of feminism say, in effect, things are not as bad in interpersonal life as feminist portraits of violence at home would have you believe, many women, and many men, say, yeah, that's right, it's not *that* bad. They say this not because they are easily duped or because they have been convinced that the problem of domestic violence has been exaggerated, but because, all too often, our descriptions of the problem have not allowed ordinary women to feel good about staying, if they feel they need to stay, or to feel good about leaving, if they feel they need to leave, or for ordinary men to feel that they can change. Whether women stay or leave, their predominant feeling is guilt. That guilt is hard to erase, I think, because it reflects an anger about having to make such choices at all.

I think that concern with the positive public reception given to critics of feminism has contributed to a defensive resistance against using ourselves as examples for public conversations about the most difficult dilemmas that women and men face in the arenas of intimacy, sexuality, and everyday life choices. We can't afford complexity, so the argument goes, when the forces allied against us are so powerful. These concerns also have amplified our fear into something near paranoia that any hesitation or ambiguity in our argument will only feed counterfeminist efforts and will undermine our position in the university, and in the wider culture. Finally, and ironically, these fears lead us to redouble efforts to reassert our own moral authority rather than engage in direct intellectual and moral debate with our opponents.

Feminists have an enormously important role to play in helping to shape public dialogue about how and for whom social opportunities are structured. To participate in this effectively we must be willing to take risks and to engage in practical discussions about the dilemmas and limitations of choice. This means, I think, being willing to consider the possibility that some of our explanations of women's realities have not felt to many women as if they had much to do with their lives or with how to improve them.

Maybe we need to practice more self-critical dialogue in school class-rooms, civic centers, popular magazines and talk shows, and even on street corners. We might find more reception for our own political and moral arguments than we think. There is ample evidence to suggest that the public has grown to accept many principles of feminism as fact. Many women and men inside and outside the academy are trying to balance complex lives that include careers, interpersonal relationships, and some joy. This ought to enable more open dialogue about the complexity and unevenness of our lives.

Yet we have to acknowledge that even this honesty will never fully protect any one of us from the unreasonable choices that we all have to face. But if facts and honesty won't protect us, then at least we might find a new way to talk about these difficult choices in public, and that conversation might help us all to create some wider options together. I think we have to take a chance. We need to be able to make judgments and to build different institutions and social systems of support based on those judgments.

So I've found myself in a curious place: I agree with neither the critics nor the defenders of feminism in any simple way. After you've existed reasonably securely for awhile, I think you have to wonder what else you have to say to justify your existence besides the fact that you have survived. Successes and failures. How much truth can we stand? What don't we know about one another? And if we do know, what don't we tell about each other? And if we do tell, what do we still try to hide from one another and the "outside" world, and why? Whom or what are we trying to protect by keeping secrets?

6 Sanctuaries

Waiting

Late June 1995. The trial was supposed to have begun already. But it's been delayed by motions *in limine,* legal disputes about the scope of admissible evidence, requests for special hearings and special jury instructions, arguments for and against admitting certain statements, records, tapes, photographs. All the necessary inquiries into what rules of law will govern the trier of fact, what instructions will define the jury's work, shape what it sees and does not see.

I've been postponing my vacation back east so that I can attend the proceedings, but I really have to decide soon whether I will be able to leave at all. The summer weeks before the semester are dwindling. I'm longing to spend warm July nights in Connecticut. Dusk; the faint murmur of trucks on a distant highway will be my companions in the woodsy seclusion of our house in Old Lyme. I imagine myself sitting on the low front porch. I will watch the angle of a setting sun crawl slowly across the surface of the lawn, glinting the leaves gold, casting the whorl of summer bugs in relief, stuck in one moment, oblivious to the utter redundancy of my watching something so complete and perfect without me.

July 7, 1995. I am at an art reception in downtown San Diego. The Colombian sculptor Doris Salcedo is here for the opening of an exhibition of her works in the Museum of Contemporary Art. It's called *Sleeper.* I wander through the rooms filled with ordinary objects of daily life. Shoes, a bed, some cloth loosely tacked on the wall with surgical thread, a rough-hewn cabinet angled in the corner. But these things aren't ordinary objects at all. It's unnerving. They've been dislocated, displaced, disturbed, like their owner; ripped like a throbbing heart from the warm body of the night by an intruder, unannounced but known, astonishing the domestic scene with a wordless violence.

The artist rises to speak.

"We must place ourselves in another's place; in the private place of violence that becomes collective because violence belongs to everyone. These objects here, they permanently scream the absence of the person who was killed. Those lost shoes, untied, abandoned, they represent the decline in the price of bananas, a person killed on the plantation because the price fell.

"No violence can be isolated from our own lives. Time is condensed, the present and the past juxtaposed, together again. She is sleeping in her bed. He is forced to get up. The bed is still warm minutes after, when he is dead. We try to erase the traces of violence the next day. But everyday objects remain, silent witnesses of a life erased."

And then I am in Andrea's bedroom. I see clothes on the floor, a brown electrical extension cord, shoes, handwritten notes, grocery lists, keys, photographs, computer disks, some jewelry, a warm bed.

"When someone is killed," Salcedo concludes, "it is in place of each of us; we should be thankful to them for dying in place of us."

I am the clothes, the cord, the shoes, the notes, the keys, the photographs, the disks, the rings, the warm bed. I cannot keep quiet. I must tell what I have seen. I must speak.

July 1995. I am still waiting. I write an editorial for the local paper about the shock and pain of the shoes, the warm bed.

"For those of us who knew Andrea—and who are about to relive her murder in more detail than we ever wanted to know ... the events of early November 1994 are becoming graphic and present again. Gathering the items of Andrea's everyday life ... we who knew her are surrounded by objects whose very existence mocks us. Meaningless and unannounced to anyone else, to us these are memories, objects [screaming] her absence."

I tell everyone I don't see her as a victim. She became a victim without ever being one. I say there is nothing given, nothing natural about victims. Or about violators. I write that everyone should have the right to live free from bodily harm.

Unsurprisingly, there are mixed reactions to the editorial. A few thank me for it. Others send me letters saying I am wrong; Andrea made bad choices. She didn't get married. Society punished her. She didn't get married to the right sort of Christian man who would know how to be self-sacrificing and nurturing, not egocentric. God punished her. She paid too much attention to feminists who filled her head with false ideas, who urged her to live outside the rules of common sense. She punished herself.

I wonder how we can all be so right.

To live free from bodily harm. It's simple, basic. A simple right. A basic need. Watch out now, careful, carry your reasons high above your head. You're walking over bodies. It's just the dead and dying. There, that was easy. Wasn't it?

Joining

The necessary eclipse of responsibility. This is what I felt in all the reactions to Andrea's death, in the questions from the press, in letters to the editor, in responses to the presentations and speeches that I made to all different sorts of groups, in discussions with friends. And I even felt it on some days in meetings of the San Diego Domestic Violence Council. A slight shifting in the seat, a clearing of the throat, a need to turn away from the bright day and rest on our laurels, tired from the wearisome vigilance of living.

I won't exempt myself from wanting to mock this penumbra of guilt brought on by haunted shoes, by the ghosts in a stranger's warm bed. Of course, I'd rather say, it has nothing to do with me. How could it? I won't deny wanting to avoid the threatening, enveloping despair that surely follows from something so simple, so stunningly stark as the thought that we share the burden for what happens in others' lives by merely not thinking about our own. I, too, would rather be bereft of memory. I, too, want the comfort of limning, once and for all, the boundaries between good and evil.

But in the insistence and repetition of all the reasons why it couldn't happen to you or to me, and in the surety of all the pronouncements about how well we are doing to prevent this theft of trust, this bereavement of freedom from bodily harm, from happening at home to ordinary, decent people like me or you, I have heard something else. Call it reasonable doubt. And I have heard in this reasonable doubt something hopeful and public: the possibility that we might yet together do more to strengthen women's sense of power and men's sense of care.

Something happened to me after Andrea was killed. I know I was searching. My name kept getting circulated in the local domestic violence community and, almost without knowing it, I decided to follow my name. I wasn't really sure what I was looking for, but I felt more and more that my work needed to be connected to some kind of material change that might improve women's lives. That was my security blanket, always has been.

One oddly humid San Diego evening in August 1995, only weeks after the trial and Andrés's conviction, I was attending a fund-raiser for WomanCare, a women's health clinic in San Diego. Then, WomanCare was one of a handful of abortion providers in the county, and the only self-identified feminist clinic in the region. My friend Ashley, who ran WomanCare, had raised the stakes in clinic funding. Sometimes she had to wear a bulletproof vest to work and stand still, dignified and pregnant, while protesters berated her for daring to conceive a child and work for women's choices with the same body. Ashley has always been a survivor. She knew the ins and outs of how to create lists of potential big donors, how to make a pitch that was bipartisan enough to offend no one, and how to make this one of the women's events of the year, not to miss.

The literati of the women's community were present in droves, grazing at the tables of hors d'oeuvres donated by the French Pastry Shop, sipping California wines and passing around business cards, waiting for the next politician to arrive. There were senators and members of the assembly from California, city councilors. Even the mayor was slated to appear.

And there was Casey Gwinn, aspiring city attorney and president of the Domestic Violence Council.

"Hi, Kathy," he said, introducing himself and his wife to me. "We talked about you today at the council meeting. We want you to join the council."

I was shocked as much that he was there at all as that he knew who I was. I thought Casey opposed abortion services, whether publicly or privately funded, on religious grounds. I figured maybe he squared that somehow with an argument about the politics of choice; or maybe it was all just politics.

"Yes," I said, "I had heard that might be a possibility. I saw Denise Frey a few days ago and said that I was willing to take the seat on the council offered to the San Diego City Commission on the Status of Women. I heard you were looking for a representative from the commission and now that I have been appointed, I'd be glad to volunteer."

"Great. Oh, and by the way, nice editorial. We're doing our big fundraiser in October. Hope to see you there." October is Domestic Violence Awareness Month. The council was planning to use the month for a variety of public awareness projects, including sponsoring a gala dinner planned at the convention center.

"I'll try to be there," I said.

Two tables filled with SDSU students attended the gala on October 12, 1995. It was one of the first indicators of how widely Andrea's death had changed the consciousness of the campus. Black tied and black gowned, the young women and men from the sororities and fraternities that had sponsored the tables listened with intensity to Assemblywoman Sheila Kuehl's speech about the everyday, ordinary lives of the women who became victims of violence and their everyday, ordinary abusers and what we in California were doing about it.

Casey Gwinn was there. And Peter Gallagher and scores of others in the community who had committed their time and resources to making a difference. Gwinn was the guest of honor, slated to be recognized by the council for his contributions to stopping the violence in women's lives. Earlier that year, in April 1995, Ann O'Dell had been honored with the council's newly named Andrea O'Donnell Award. Lesley had been there for that occasion.

Still, October 12, 1995, was an odd evening. Only three days before, sheriffs had found English-Howard, gagged and shrouded, hanging in his cell.

I joined the San Diego Domestic Violence Council and spent two and a half years on it as an at-large member of the board, a sort of minister without portfolio, broadly representing the women's community as a not-too-silent witness. The council has been in existence in some form or another longer than almost any other domestic violence–related community-based group in the United States. It's well known, highly regarded, and powerful. If you want to be active in this field in San Diego, you need the blessing of the council.

Early on I found myself uncertain about my role. I had come to this group without the credentials of any real street work in the field. There was definitely a pecking order. No surprises there. Here were folks who had been working for years on a topic that had only recently galvanized me. I wasn't an attorney or a licensed social worker, I lacked the perspective of the probation officer or the shelter worker or administrator or member of law enforcement; I wasn't a judge or a city government worker. But I sat among this powerful and influential group for many months and tried to help figure out what we were doing.

Pretty soon I settled into being a kind of gadfly among the professional practitioners who populated the committees and executive positions. I spent some time on the data collection committee and learned a lot about uncoordinated crime statistics, about emerging death review teams and what we don't know about the shelter population. I spent some time with different folks in the treatment and training committee, reviewing the materials that are used to train the trainers and trying to bring a different political perspective into the process. I worked briefly planning one of the conferences that occur every October. I helped for a while with the strategic planning process for the council. And I found that my sometimes naïve questions caused trouble. I suppose that's all right though; someone's got to stir the pot from time to time.

But the hook for me was always Andrea. Not just Andrea, but the Andreas who were still among us. It had hardly been a year since Andrea was killed. On campus, many students who knew her well had planned ways to memorialize her life. Donations to the women's studies scholarship fund named after her were coming in consistently from all over the country, and the department planned to make the first scholarship award the following spring. A group was working to rename the Women's Resource Center the Andrea O'Donnell Women's Resource Center. Another group was arranging a music fest in her honor. Another worked on the Take Back the Night March.

Others who hardly knew her still felt the need to act. One graduate student who had conducted a survey of the campus's response to violence against women approached me to figure out how to do more. Her work helped garner the support of a group of administrators, students, and faculty, and we changed the university's policy and protocols on sexual and intimate violence. Finally, a group of students who had been in my women and politics class the semester of Andrea's death joined several other graduate students who had been shocked into action by her loss to work on a research project I was helping shape.

For several years, the topic of women's health had been center stage in California politics. Republican and Democratic women were determined to remain as bipartisan as possible during California governor Pete Wilson's years when it came to critical women's issues, issues that they thought knew no party lines. Issues like breast cancer and domestic violence. The California Women's Health Project grew out of that strategy. Supported by funding from the James Irvine Foundation, the project was run by the California Elected Women's Association for Education and Research. CEWAER, which claims to be the nation's oldest and largest association of elected women officials, is a highly regarded, decidedly effective networking and research group designed to get women into public office and keep them there, and keep the public's eye on women's needs no matter which party is in power.

In 1995, Dede Alpert was the president of CEWAER. Then a California assemblywoman from District 78 in San Diego, and now a state senator, Alpert has always been an outstanding and outspoken advocate for laws that will help stop domestic violence. Following on the heels of CEWAER's study of the scope of the public health threat of domestic violence in the state, she was eager to have San Diego be the site for an evaluation of regional preventative and intervention services offered to women victims of violence. I got a call in July 1995 from her office to help launch the investigation. I got in touch with Claudia Hergesheimer, a young woman graduate student from the School of Social Work who was interested in the field and, with the assistance of Alpert's office, Claudia coordinated the research process.

San Diego has long been regarded as a model community because of its innovative, multidisciplinary approach to domestic violence intervention. You can't go anywhere without hearing that San Diego has been a pathbreaker. Beside Duluth, Minnesota, San Diego ranks among the top cities in the country for community-based integrated responses. I suppose it deserves this reputation. Aggressive prosecution policies, cooperation from law enforcement, a long history of a women's community politicizing the issue, all these and more have had symbolic and practical effect. But the survey gave us pause.

First, it showed us how difficult it is to get information from service providers if you ask for it at the wrong time of year and if the organizations do not have the data organized in the way you need them.

"I don't understand what's wrong," Claudia said one afternoon when we were meeting to review her time line. "I mean, we got everyone's buy-in at the planning meeting in September; they helped shape the questions, and now it's like pulling teeth to get the answers back."

"Look, we'll go with what we have. It will be more anecdotal. You wouldn't be able to do the statistical correlations you might have wanted if the numbers are too low. But even the information that we are getting is important, and even the fact that it's hard to get the information is significant."

It was near December, near the holidays, when, for shelters especially, time is at a premium. We got about a 40 percent response rate from the 103 organizations in San Diego we surveyed who provide some kind of service to victims of violence against women. We wanted more, but it was not a bad rate. But we found out more about what we don't and can't know than anything else.

We were trying to get demographic data. Yet many organizations couldn't access the data either because they weren't available or because there were too few staff to collate them. You'd be surprised at the number of shelters and advocacy organizations operating with only the most rudimentary computer capacity. Caseloads are logged and sorted, but, in most organizations, there is no one available to enter the data into any electronic form. They're just too busy staying alive.

Mistrust still exists among the different constituencies serving victims and offenders. The result is that most of the collaboration that does take place, outside of the council's own meetings, is among groups who share common goals and objectives. So law enforcement and legal services work more closely with each other than they do with educational institutions; professionals in shelter communities and clinical communities still display residual distrust of law enforcement's response. At least that's the law enforcement perspective.

Individual relationships can transcend some of these tensions, but there is a lot more work to be done to build trust among the various community groups working in the field. And the council knows it.

We spent almost a year debating and negotiating an offer made by the San Diego County Public Health Office and the County Board of Supervisors to establish a Primary Prevention Council designed to focus on deterrence. There were concerns with motive, concerns with control, concerns with recognition. After public debates and hearings, memoranda and minutes of meetings cascading across the county in a torrent of words and paper, the project seemed almost certain to be derailed. Then it got back on track. The county and the council agreed to work together on prevention within the structure of the council.

I guess the fact that suspicion and distrust coexist with a desire to work together doesn't strike me as so odd anymore. It's the same tensions, the same conflicts between belonging and independence that you see in the intimate relationships we all work so hard to repair. We want to love and be loved, we want to give and receive recognition, we want to be strong and powerful and autonomous and caring. And why should we have to choose?

Explaining

There is precious little accurate data about the scope or pattern of violence in intimate relations. One thing we do know: intimate violence knows no limitations of class, race, age, religion, or sexuality; it lacks understanding of the simplest academic lessons about how demography is supposed to limit individual opportunity. It punishes rich and poor alike, folks of every color and class and religion and sexuality, for trusting one another, for sleeping in the same bed with someone who can harm them. Like Andrea did.

It isn't as simple as choosing the right partner for life and marrying him or her. People change; even if you're in a marriage and devoted to staying in it, you might find yourself changing too. Doing things you never thought you could do. You'll find that you feel weak. You'll even talk to yourself; you'll say, "I should know better." And, "He's really loving sometimes, you know. Really sweet." And you mean it. And he is.

But the longer you stay, the more you get used to it. You can't trust yourself not to get used to it. You can't trust yourself.

There's even some evidence that long-term psychological or physical abuse changes brain function. Stress-induced neurochemical changes occur in the part of the brain called the hippocampus, where memory is stored; beaten-in habits of mind develop that anchor you in place by allowing you to forget, flattening your emotions, temporarily extinguishing your fear. You lose perspective; you can't remember what just happened. There, there, that's better. It's a handy neural coping mechanism.

But not for long. Your body leaks; you seem to get these headaches so strong they make you want to sleep. Strange, ugly flashbacks interrupt an ordinary day with images you wouldn't dare whisper to your best friend. A clap of thunder, a slammed door, the smell of a certain food, a vase of flowers, rattled kitchen implements. These might leave you breathless, shivering with an unspecified fear right in the middle of the day. It's like combat. The all-pervasive effects are hard to get away from.

It isn't as simple as predicting the future from the past. We can graph a cycle of violence in some families; we can see how old habits are hard to break. But we cannot say, finally, that there are easy ways to discover who will be a victim and who will not. Even if certain parts of the victim's past are horrific, we have no litmus test for telling the future. Even if we know that one-third to one-half of battered women report a history of childhood abuse, and even if we know that perpetrators report even higher rates of witnessing abuse as a child, or of being abused themselves, it's hard to take comfort in correlations.

Because how do correlations breed hope? What kind of hope springs from being lucky enough to have been born on the right side of the equation? Should we feel hopeless if we're not? And even if we think that something like what happened to Andrea and Andrés will never happen to us, will we sleep comfortably, blanketed by statistics, safe and warm and snug in our scientifically secured beds, the next time we read the headlines, the next time we hear the neighbors say, just like they said about Andrea and Andres, But they were such a happy, loving couple? Sure, they had their problems, but who doesn't?

There are no fail-safe indicators of risk. Neither having witnessed domestic violence as a child nor having been battered before allows us to differentiate without hesitation between those who are now being beaten in their homes and those who are not. We cannot say simply, once and for all, once a victim, always a victim. Or even once a batterer, always a batterer.

Escaping abuse isn't as simple as having enough money or marketable skills. Remember Dr. C. There is no doubt that it's much more difficult for women with few economic and social resources to leave an abuser. In fact, the likelihood of leaving increases with financial independence. But money and resources alone cannot guarantee autonomy. The overwhelming majority of women who leave their abusers are financially self-supporting. But so are more than half of the women who stay with partners who have been abusive.

And the booze and the drugs and the mobility and the lack of empathy and the inability to communicate and the neglect and the hostility and the immaturity, all the retrospective signals found in those who abuse, it's hard to know what to do with all that we know. Go on. Get out your score-card. Check your partner, rate your relationship. Did you expect what you found? Do you see your husband, your friend, your lover, your son, your daughter there? Did you want to finally, furiously, insist that they're different? So did Andrea. So did Andrés.

So we know one more thing from all this statistically probable lack of clarity—knowing that there are no stable boundaries, no simple, mappable geography of intimate violence, tells us almost nothing about how differently we each might deal with violence if and when it occurs in the middle of our lives. Because even if it isn't as simple as choosing the right partner and staying married forever, or getting past the age of thirty-five, the age before which the risks are greater, or having enough money to save your life; even if you've been lucky enough never to have been one of the millions of abused children, or the millions of others who have watched their fathers and maybe their mothers, bored and drunk on a Saturday night, throwing fists in the air, or bottles, or statues, seeing them land on loved faces; and even if you've never overindulged, never not listened, never shouted at the moon with your pain; even if you're just as normal as the rest of us—can you be so sure you won't one day become a statistic, almost a cipher, without a name?

These two facts—that both violence and our responses to it are countryless nomads, enterprises without boundaries—combine to mean that our analyses of cause and our interventions against effect are about as predictably reliable as the weather report. (And, yes, I know the theories about the seasons of violence.)

There is no one to blame for this unpredictability of cause and effect. Not really. It's only been since the 1970s that the issue of "wife" battering has even had a name. Of course, now we describe this crime as domestic violence, bracketing again its public nature with a simple twist of vocabulary. There are many who want to call it domestic abuse, or even to collapse it back into the general category of crimes against the person out of which it was carved a short time ago. But that's a different story.

In this short period of time since the problem has had a name, women—and it has been mostly a women's self-help enterprise, until recently—women have been trying simply to stay alive, safe and alive.

Maybe we haven't been spending as much time counting and measuring and weighing as we should have.

There is no *one* to blame, because it's a conspiracy of gaps and absences, absences and gaps, which have grown like a slowly widening fault line right in the middle of the desert.

There are still far too few shelters. Fewer than for stray animals or re-cycled paper or used shoes. Funding for intervention is tight and very bureaucratically controlled; funding for prevention is even tighter. Most public money still goes to the first line of defense for women—the cops and sheriffs who can arrest, who can take away your abuser, in some cases even over your protests.

The law enforcement and legal systems were the first in this country to reform their ways of dealing with violence against women through more aggressive arrest and prosecution policies. They still have a long way to go to institutionalize these changes. And whether reforms, such as mandated prosecution, should be institutionalized is still being debated.

If you live in Alexandria, Virginia; Baltimore, Maryland; Brooklyn, New York; Denver, Colorado; Duluth, Minnesota; King County, Wash-ington; Los Angeles, California; San Diego, California; or in Florida, Minnesota, New Jersey, Texas, or Utah, the debate is more or less over, for now. City or district attorneys' offices in these jurisdictions operate under differing degrees of pro-prosecution or so-called "no drop" policies. In some cases this means that you have no choice about pressing charges; if you call 911 and tell the police operator that you are being beaten in your home, the city or district attorney takes over, charging and prosecuting your abuser even if you refuse to cooperate.

The fissures and absences extend to knowing what policies are most effective. Three-fourths of the San Diego providers who responded to our survey said that they did no formal evaluation of their programs; most who evaluated anything used lack of recidivism or reports of client satisfaction as indicators of success.

There have been no national studies of which arrest and prosecution approaches work best. We're not even sure how to measure success. Does a higher rate of conviction necessarily mean that potential victims are more protected? Are we sure that the lower rates of domestic violence–related homicides are the result of more aggressive prosecution policies?

Between 1985 and 1994, San Diego reported a significant drop in the number of DV homicides, from thirty to seven. Andrea was murdered in 1994 and was included in those statistics. Hers was defined as a DV homicide. The disturbingly odd thing is, though, that Andrés had been arrested in San Diego before. About 3:15 A.M. on June 3, 1994, English-Howard had been arrested for possessing a small amount of crack cocaine. The charges were dropped.

We're not sure about the most effective way to treat batterers either. Programs for batterers compete with one another for funding and for clients before they can prove the effectiveness of their interventions. When you work in the field you can feel an ever-present tension. Almost approaching panic, there's a palpable urgency to keep all the parts of the treatment machine moving, keep the batterers moving through, make sure everything is turning; it's as if perpetual motion is what it's really all about.

So we don't know much about recidivism among batterers who have completed treatment programs, about whether rates of reabuse are significantly decreased or essentially the same. We don't have this information because, in part, there is the frightful urgency that there are always more men (it's almost always men) to get through the system. And in regions like San Diego, conviction rates are increased by the availability of probation as an option for an offender who agrees to treatment in a mandatory yearlong program. There are a lot of dollars at stake in treatment.

We also still lack accurate data about the role that medical authorities can and should play in community intervention programs. Not everyone agrees with the mandatory reporting of those recorded wounds, the bruises and burns and lacerations logged in otherwise confidential medical records. Medical authorities aren't adequately trained about how to elicit information from women who come into their offices or clinics with complaints. And without adequate escape routes for the woman, the combination of mandatory medical reporting and mandatory prosecution sends chills down the spines of some of the most ardent victim advocates.

Yet, because medical evidence is still so critical to establishing the veracity of a complaint, especially with a less than cooperative victim, you can understand why many advocates want to require doctors to report what they know. Especially if prosecution is the name of the game. Especially since successful prosecution creates the sense that we have responded to abuse adequately and with some finality by punishing the individual responsible for the crime.

Apart from media campaigns, prevention programs are almost nonexistent. It took a lot of persistence and dedication for the San Francisco–based Family Violence Protection Fund to get its black-and-blue billboards and posters about domestic violence decorating California roadways and bus stops—images of the domestic monotony of broken glass and shadowy, threatening gestures that nevertheless fill the pictured room with fearful shouts. Invading the everyday with the everyday, cautionary reminders of something most people don't want to see on their way to work or traveling home from the grocery store, these images were powerful in their ordinariness.

There has been enormous resistance to anything like to a coherent, systematic educational campaign about domestic violence. Only a few public school districts have been able to integrate age-appropriate education about violence in intimate relationships into their curriculum, and then usually only for sessions of a week or two. Wouldn't want to scare the children. Sex and violence in U.S. society are both omnipresent and nowhere in our public life.

Finally, for all the much-vaunted discussion of a multidisciplinary response to intimate violence, I see a notable absence of community in our community response. Each faction of shelter workers, law enforcement and legal advocates, health professionals, judicial and probation officers, and treatment providers spends so much time leveraging its meager resources and trying to garner wider public support that it is easy to forget about the women who really do depend upon our cooperation and coherence to make it to the next day. And this happens, I think, not because of malicious dissension or high-mindedness or even egoism, though there is of course some of those, but because we all have more or less gotten caught up in the day-to-day business of survival.

In the 1970s, the battered women's movement inaugurated shifts of key in the register of how we define and work against intimate violence. Stressing the structural nature of the problem shifted the blame from the individual onto social systems (such as private, nuclear families) that entrapped individuals in deadly games of gambit with no exit. Advocacy meant working not only to enable any individual woman to survive, but also to engage the public in an assessment and accounting of violence in the home. Much of that altered register has been muted, for some very complicated reasons.

As late as 1994, the year that Andrea was killed, there had been no sys-tematic investigation of the extent to which advocacy was widely shared or even understood by practitioners in the field. The one national survey of domestic violence providers that exists concluded that most practitioners defined advocacy in terms of achieving immediate objectives as opposed to long-term goals; they stressed working with individuals over structural change. These results were mirrored in our study of San Diego in 1995.

Yet the most compelling reason for the myopia of our theories and prac-tices is that the explanations we have come to expect (and without which we feel uncomfortable) conspire to keep us from dealing with the obvious, which we should be able to see all around us but insist on explaining away. At the heart of all our efforts to locate the uncommon variables that explain violence, to identify the correlates of abuse in clear, crisp equations of prob-ability and cause, to label victims into neat categories and box them and put them on the shelf, and to punish offenders surely and swiftly, we are quietly trying to push responsibility away from ourselves.

But this is crazy, you're saying. We're really only trying to see who is most at risk, trying to provide safety nets for our daughters and our sons, trying to be fair but, yes, necessarily yes, we are punishing offenders. I don't disagree with any of that. Only accidents and memories have driven me past the point of seeing the story only one way or the other.

The thing that catches me up again and again is the enormous energy we invest in proving that neither the victim nor the victimizer is one of us. Might have been, but no longer is. Now it's them, not us. And we want to be especially sure you can tell the two apart. Only accidents and memories have made me feel that most of us want to keep our distance from the very real and very painful fact that what is happening to those people over there is not infectious, is not a disease, and yet is as common as a cold; it comes out of ordinary conflicts, things we all feel, from time to time, about want-ing to love without having to let go one bit of our own tight grasp around the world.

So the more we keep the question of responsibility squarely on someone else's shoulders, the more we avoid taking a long, hard look at the unrea-sonable things we all ask one another to do but never want to or expect to have to do ourselves. Like choose between love and power.

Be responsible and choose, we say. Choose between a tattered love and an uncertain autonomy. Choose between a careless affection, a rock-hard, quixotic fierceness, and a sense of freedom as ephemeral as a dream. And, to be certain that you show us you are capable of choice, make sure you choose without support, without the security of knowing whether the choice is right, without any of the comforts that any of us would surely demand for ourselves before we choose. Because if you can choose that way, without support and with finality, then we'll be forced to admit that you really are free. But if you can't, well, then we'll feel reassured. The simple knowledge and sheer visibility of your own failure to choose wisely will be enough to comfort us that, unlike you, we would know what to do.

Yet each of us knows, if she or he would only admit it, that we lack those comforts, that security, that we need others to help us through the quagmire and confusion of choices we never want to make. So when we say "I would know what to do," it may be that those words are the only harbor in which we can hide, the only refuge we can take from the very real, half-imagined fear that we might not know, that we might not be any different from Andrea. Or Andrés.

Only accidents and memories, only the used shoes and the warm bed, have gotten me to think that we have been expecting each other to make behavioral sea changes with very little acknowledgment about how hard the so-called choices really are to make. The more empowered you feel, the more the choices are yours, yours to make all alone. After all, that's what makes you feel empowered in the first place, isn't it?

Just like Andrea.

Living

Every November the students at the Andrea O'Donnell Women's Resource Center host a music fest. It's a fund-raising event for the scholarship named in her honor, a scholarship dedicated to assist students who choose an activist path to support them through their college careers. This November was no different.

I sent Andrea's mother, Lesley, the notice about this year's event. A few weeks passed. Then I got a letter that shocked me back into the reality of all the pain that she continues to suffer day after day of remembering her daughter's death.

She was upset by having read some of the things I had written, she said. I hadn't gotten the story just right, she said. Hadn't captured the essence of Andrea, of what she had been all about.

I don't know why I was surprised by her reaction. I shouldn't have been. It's not just a matter of fact, this living and dying. It's not just a simple matter of getting the dates and the names right.

I hope that we will always be separated from one another by some margin of error. Call it a buffer, call it a safe, bearable distance for the soul's peace of mind. It's what allows us to risk, I guess, getting close enough to hurt one another, and then stopping just short of doing that; we get as close as we can and then stop in that safe, buffered zone we call love.

Not a safe house, where women hide, walled in, waiting, hoping for deliverance. Not safe-kept, safe-guarded, alone with all the others. But a sanctuary, enabled by the power of risk, controlled by the power of love.

I have wanted to convey the message that violence can hit anyone. There may be things that we can do to be alert to its dynamic, there may be ways to recognize the ordinary vices that exacerbate its growth and development. There may even be some legitimacy to the sorts of behavioral cues that advocates who have dealt with this for years have used to help read the warning signs.

But, more than anything, I have wanted to make it clear that even strong women can become victims.

This is not a simple message. If violence can happen to anyone, it's not because all women are potential victims or all men potential batterers, but because choice is a full-time responsibility that cannot be undertaken all alone. No matter how empowered any one of us feels, no matter how aware, how informed, how knowledgeable, being in control of our lives and being informed are not individual acts. They are public projects.

An Epilogue of Sorts
There have been many women who have inspired me to continue despite the obstacles I have faced; I hope one day to be an inspiration for someone else.

—Andrea O'Donnell, 1994

And Andrea, you have been. You have done what you wanted to do. Inspired. Breathed into the world. Breathed in and out and into the world; your life. Shown yourself in the world with the incandescent eloquence of mystery; your hopes. Wrenched us past all the limits of despair, past the willfulness of power, and made us stand finally on a bare, beautiful land and say that we have nothing more to save us from the world; your love.

And knowing that love won't save us, or power, or hope. Only living will. Finally, we can live by taking up our place among all those others who have started to breathe in and out and into the world and without whom we cannot even imagine being alive. Without all those others.

I see you staring at us, the living. But I am no longer afraid when I hear your laughter unexpectedly on an autumn night; when I see the glint of your eyes reflected in a turquoise gem, in the curve of a silver pin, slightly arched, I can smile now.

From time to time, I still wish that you were here. And Andrés too; yes, and Andrés too.

But in any of those thin, still mournful moments of yearning to erase the past and start time all over again, you remind me of what is already here, already with me.

My two sons, men now, are before me, breathing in the world. I see them. They are so different. And that is good. One, all willowy wiry arms and spindly legs, sprouted manly in the recent year, still nearly wordlessly reflective, absorbs and waits and quietly reaches out and fashions himself as a philosopher, asking why and how of the world. The other, audaciously muscular and extravagantly effusive, studies all types and their speeches, echoes the words of the great and the small, moves chameleon-like among the centuries, crafting his craft, and shows to all and sundry the emotions we use to build and to break one another—an actor, a storyteller.

I watch them both, each in his own way, find a manly way to care. I know that I have helped them find their ways into the world; I have helped them understand the comfort of a loving touch, the need for tender mercies, the strength of kindness. And I have helped them know that they are not alone. I know that they have learned all these things together because they tell me not to worry, they tell me to let them go into the world, breathing in and out.

And I am not alone. And my love, she watches with me.

All of us, already here, in the world, in the middle of our own lives, together.

Credits and Resources

~

Some of the sources used for the research cited in chapter 6 are Dennis Charney, Ariel Deutch, John Krystal, Steven Southwick, and Michael Davis, "Psychobiologic Mechanisms of Posttraumatic Stress Disorder," *Archives of General Psychiatry* 50 (1993): 294–303; Cheryl Hanna, "No Right to Choose: Mandated Victim Participation in Domestic Violence Prosecutions," *Harvard Law Review* 109 (1996): 1850–1910; and Einat Peled and Jeffrey L. Edelson, "Advocacy for Battered Women: A National Survey," *Journal of Family Violence* 9 (1994): 285–296.

There are a growing number of agencies on the local, national, and international level that provide support for victims of domestic violence. Most communities in the United States have domestic violence councils that are multidisciplinary—representing a variety of agencies of prevention and intervention—and community based.

In the United States, there is a twenty-four-hour hotline for victims of abuse who need shelter or other support: 1-800-799-7233. The Family Violence Prevention Fund is a nonprofit organization that focuses on domestic violence education, prevention, and public policy reform. Call 800-END-ABUSE. The fund also can be contacted at www.igc.org/fund. Additional resources can be found through the Minnesota Center against Voilence and Abuse (MINCAVA) at www.mincava.umn.edu.

International information is available through the United Nations, Office of the UN Special Rapporteur on Violence against Women, ICES, 2, Kynsey Terrace, Colombo 8, Sri Lanka; tel, (941) 685085/698048; fax, (941) 698048; e-mail, ices_cmb@sri.lanka.net (attn: Lisa Kois), and also through Womankind in the United Kingdom, through Brita Schmidt, brita@womankind.org.uk.

Kathleen B. Jones is professor of women's studies and former associate dean of the College of Arts and Letters at San Diego State University. She is the award-winning author of *Compassionate Authority: Democracy and the Representation of Women*. She is co-editor, with Anna Jónasdóttir, of *The Political Interests of Gender* and, with Cathy Cohen and Joan Tronto, of *Women Transforming Politics*. Jones is an activist-scholar who has served on the City of San Diego Commission on the Status of Women, which she also represented on the San Diego Domestic Violence Council, and is a past cochair of the San Diego Violence against Women Task Force.